On Both Sides of the
IRON CURTAIN

For Dorothy Roman

Wanda has told me that
Learning is very important to you
I hope you will find my book
interesting and useful.

Israel Helms
6090 Bella Vista Drive
Fort Mohave, AZ 86426
928-7882660
helms@npgcable.com.

On Both Sides of the
IRON CURTAIN

THE STORY OF A RUSSIAN
REFUGEE IN AMERICA

ISRAEL HELMS

TATE PUBLISHING *& Enterprises*

Tate Publishing
& Enterprises

Tate Publishing is committed to excellence in the publishing industry. Our staff of highly trained professionals, including editors, graphic designers, and marketing personnel, work together to produce the very finest books available. The company reflects the philosophy established by the founders, based on Psalms 68:11,

"The Lord Gave The Word And Great Was The Company Of Those Who Published It."

If you would like further information, please contact us:
1.888.361.9473 | www.tatepublishing.com
Tate Publishing & Enterprises, llc | 127 E. Trade Center Terrace
Mustang, Oklahoma 73064 USA

On Both Sides of the Iron Curtain

The opinions expressed by the author are not necessarily those of Tate Publishing, LLC.

This book is designed to provide accurate and authoritative information with regard to the subject matter covered. This information is given with the understanding that neither the author nor Tate Publishing, LLC is engaged in rendering legal, professional advice. Since the details of your situation are fact dependent, you should additionally seek the services of a competent professional.

Book design copyright © 2007 by Tate Publishing, LLC. All rights reserved.
Cover design by Lindsay B. Behrens
Interior design by Leah LeFlore

Published in the United States of America
ISBN: 978-1-598867-1-0-7

07.02.26

•••

For my grandsons, Mark and Jacob,
my two diamonds—so brilliant, so
different, so kind, and so precious

•••

acknowledgments

I am in debt to all my friends, who took great personal responsibility to awaken incessant writing ambitions in a man of very prosaic occupation. Now, as Pandora's Box is open, I am grateful to them for not leaving me out in the cold. I thank everyone who took time to go through the manuscript of my story to see if it's readable or digestible. Instead, they were too kind to find it "smooth, captivating, honest and informative." These good friends are Andy and Linda Andrechyn, Dotty Fenner, Tom Fitzpatrick, Ben Haney, Hope Hays, Ray Keller, Maggie Milton, Michael and Sofia Schiller, and also many others who listened to some of the true fragments of my story, giving me this "open mouth" look of curiosity and encouraging me to put my story in writing.

I am particularly grateful to my daughter Nora, who was my first confidant, and to my grandsons, Jacob and Mark, who got so excited with prospect of their "Deda" going public with his story that they didn't know where to put an excess of their overflowing admiration. Has anyone tried to make a bubble bath in the running whirlpool? That's exactly what it was. I want you guys to know—all love and admiration is mine.

Mom and Dad, you made me what I am, with all my hunger for goodness, knowledge and love. From where you are now, you have sent me this Good Angel, protecting me in my challenging life. I love you, and I thank you for that.

This book has been to equal degree driven by two opposite sets of emotions:

the gratitude for the good, and indignation at the evil. In this sense, to be fair, I must recognize several totalitarian villains of 20th Century, their direct role in the world's horrendous turmoil and suffering. Without their "theoretical" and practical contribution, the life on our planet would be "too easy and too happy," and I would hardly have much to say in my book.

I also have to recognize a contribution of so called "Conscientious Objectors," "Secular Progressives" and other similar left wing movements in Western World. They have been very instrumental in creating a great deal of confusion in a public view of the world war against terrorism and other forms of totalitarianism. Without their effort, this war of Good against Evil would look "too straight forward and simple." And I probably would lack sufficient set of emotions to drive my writing ambitions.

foreword

When I first met Israel Helms I was impressed by his humility, graciousness, and intelligence. This first impression was expanded as I learned more about him, learned more from him, and learned to appreciate the knowledge he brings to his adopted country, the United States of America. When he asked me to write this foreword to his book, I felt honored. When you have completed your reading of this fascinating journey, I am sure your image of the difficulties of being a citizen from the oppressive political system of mid-twentieth century Russia will be indelible on your mind. You, as the reader, will also realize the practical difficulties, along with the joy, of an immigrant's assimilation into our country.

Israel Helms represents "an aging group of Russian émigrés to the West." This group combines an experience of growing up under Stalin's "self-gobbling breed of Communism, (being) brushed by the deadly winds of the Nazi invasion, and living for an extended period of time in both the Eastern European and the Western worlds." The author provides a picture of the dazzling social, philosophical and political developments of his time, and takes you with him to the "kitchen" of high technology development in his field in both Russia and the United States. Additionally, this author's experience of "writing scientific articles, writing descriptions of the engineering systems that he has designed," and the "translation of foreign patents and technical literature" between Russian and English, offers a baseline for him to relate to you, in simple terms, the technical inserts in this book.

Rarely does a reader have an opportunity to vicariously experience the personal feelings of an individual who lived almost through the whole cycle of this crucial-to-our-civilization period of history. Although this person, Jay Khmelinsky, is fictional, his journey includes many similar events experienced by the author of this book. These experiences helped mold his character into the American patriot he is today. The message he is conveying, with his description of his hero's journey, is that "to ignore the lessons of history, (leaders) are often destined to make tragic mistakes, sometimes fatal enough to cost millions of lives and cause terrible suffering for many generations." I have heard him say "the knowledge of this phenomenon by the world citizenry is also cyclical. Every new generation starts from a clean sheet, almost completely unaware of, or aloof to the consequences of ignorance in history, and is desperately in need to be reeducated."

I encourage everyone interested in modern history to enjoy your journey into the life of the hero in this fascinating book; the proud and strong man who personifies the feelings of many immigrants to our great country. As we all know, this country was founded on immigrants; and it has been, and continues to be, the most successful country in the world in assimilation of this passionate group of people.

Despite of incredibly busy and powerful factual content, this book is very easy to read. It has grasp of a thriller combined with smooth and rhythmic flow of a poem. Great humor, sometimes sarcastic, sometimes gentle, often self-directed, helps to get through both the horrendous historic events and everyday family life with equal ease. The masterful use of parables highlights the story with delicious flavor. The reader almost feels a presence of storyteller, sitting right across the coffee table, speaking to him in a simple and colorful English with a "cute" Russian accent.

Dotty Fennel
Henderson, Nevada
May 8, 2006

introduction

"In order to make a compelling point I must sometimes offer an insight or example from my personal experience."

JOHN KASICH

At my 70th I represent a group of Russian émigrés to the West, fairly unique even for this rapidly vanishing generation. That is the group which combines an experience to have grown up under Stalin's self-gobbling breed of Communism, been brushed by deadly winds of Nazi invasion, lived for extended period of time in both East European and Western worlds, and taken a little glimpse of dazzling technological, philosophical and political developments of 21st Century. As one could see, the chance for this group to speak wouldn't last long, and an opportunity for it to be heard would soon be lost. And perhaps a couple of words of wisdom will vanish with it into eternity.

In my engineering experience I was involved in writing of scientific articles—description of the engineering systems I had designed—as well as foreign patents and technical literature I had translated. I'm not a professional writer in a broad sense, and although an avid reader, I never contemplated getting involved in a book writing activity.

Upon my emigration to the United States, I often shared with my friends some episodes of my fairly unique life on both sides of the Iron Curtain. When new war, a war against Islamo-Fascism—the one that is not less, if not more, dangerous than any we went through—slammed into our door, I reflected on my life again. I was amazed at how stubborn history was in coming back with a vengeance. I was there in Russia, and I learned a lot about American modern history as well. It's the same struggle between good and evil; freedom and slavery; the connected to the world or disconnected from it; those following their conscience or indoctrinated by the power hungry villains. Only this time we are dealing with invisible army of fanatics, looking for death as the way to get out of their misery. *Armed with weapons of mass destruction, they would be in the position to take the whole civilization with them, replacing it with the wasteland and land of horror.* We are not talking here just about some temporary loss of our freedoms. We are talking now about a world that we wouldn't want our children to live in, period. Each time my listeners asked me why I wouldn't write the book about my experience and my convictions, I wondered: "Would anyone be interested?" But quite often I looked into the eyes of my listeners and read some healthy sign of curiosity. So, I decided to try.

The real dilemma for me was choice of language. My adult life was almost equally divided between two tongues: Russian of my younger adult years, and predominantly English of my mature time. Although Classic Russian of Pushkin and Tolstoy, which I sucked with the milk of my mother, would never fade from my mind, the iron slang of Bolshevik Revolution and Stalinism became a relic now. And the modern Russian has largely passed me by during my twenty-eight years in America. The question is now: "Am I comfortable enough in both classic and modern aspects of English? Would I be able to convey its spirit without sounding hollow?" So I took my chances in this aspect as well, and I'm humbly asking for reader's patience and leniency. As a modest compensation for the reader's suffering, I promise to bitter and butter my story up with some portion of sour pepper juice. That is something I had plenty of opportunity to accumulate, first, genetically, after my ancestors were kicked out of Palestine and spread all over the place by Romans two thousand years ago; and then recently in Russia, in person, under the most brutal and ridiculous, perverse and pervasive ideology the human race ever invented and put upon itself—the Communism.

We discussed the issues touched in this book on numerous occasions in bits and pieces, having some fun around the family table or over the phone. We have not always been in agreement, but we respected each other's honest perspectives and opinions. In most cases, it was friendly duel between young innocent and idealistic hearts on one hand, and the accumulated wisdom of the older generation on the other. So I finally decided to put together some details of my life and background surrounding me at different stages of my *non-allegorical* boyhood, youth and maturity. I would combine it with lifetime experience of some of my friends of the same generation, and see what the reader would say about the resulted character and philosophy of my hero.

When I shared my writing aspirations with my family and friends, I found them surprisingly excited. After they saw my first draft—the version I didn't like anyway—I found them more and more involved and instrumental. As a result, I can't claim myself a single author anymore. I would gladly acknowledge anyone involved as a co-author ... of course if I am allowed to *stick* with my worldview.

This adventure also served a very selfish purpose. I found the writing to be a process so incredibly creative and enjoyable that it could easily compete with any of my other projects in design engineering and science. It helped to recall my own life in almost snowball fashion, the way I would never expect. On top of everything, I found the writing process to be a perfect "un-boggling" tool when I didn't know what to do with my mind. It's much better than worry beads or chewing gum.

Many famous philosophers of all times maintained that history has a tendency to repeat itself; that our civilization, as anything else, develops in a fashion of dialectic spiral. It always comes back in stubborn cycles, often times on a more complicated and even more ominous level. Some people and their leaders, with propensity to ignore lessons of history, are often destined to make tragic mistakes, sometimes fatal enough to cost millions of lives and cause terrible suffering for many generations.

This phenomenon of the mass amnesia is also cyclical. Every new generation starts from a clean sheet, almost completely unaware of, or aloof to, the consequences of ignorance in history; therefore, it is desperately in need to be reeducated. I am making this idea the *leitmotif of my story*. To remind the reader over and over again about lessons of history, based on my very real personal experience and an experience of my generation, is the major purpose of my book. I call the reader to trust material presented by my hero, and to draw his own conclusions. But one thing I can't promise—to be "cool" about pervasive tendencies in the world community to ignore these lessons. I apologize in advance to some of my readers who would find me too repetitive, too "cyclical" on this particular subject, and I'm grateful in advance to anyone who would find my story revealing and convincing.

The social and political background of the book contains the well known historical facts. My hero, Jay Khmelinsky, presented them diligently to the best of his ability and led the reader to draw parallels with his own realities. Again, his life story was not a biography of one particular person, but rather a combined character of some of my friends of similar background and generation. On many occasions, though, Jay was gracious enough to step into my shoes. In turn, I let myself be in his shoes for a while. Structurally, in the main parts of the story, I asked Jay to speak for himself. But in the "Epilogue" I have intruded again, in person, with all my vengeance and passion toward my favorite "leitmotif."

Of course, I would be the most grateful storyteller in the world if you find a single paragraph in my book to take your busy time off and think some more about what we are up against. If you, however, find nothing of value but this Russian accent of mine, which some of my friends consider "cute," that's all right, too—I still hope to talk to you about that later. So let me now share a "microphone" with Jay, my good friend and associate in this modest endeavor.

chapter 1

"A simple way to take measure of a country is to look at how many want in ... and how many want out."

TONY BLAIR

I was the last in line of refugees leaving Russia for good the morning of May 19, 1977. My daughter Lora and son-in-law Bob were ahead of me, closing their suitcases after search. My two suitcases were both open on the table. The burly custom officer at Moscow International Airport was thoroughly enjoying himself. The officer was not in any hurry. He slowly and methodically emptied the neatly packed suitcases. He picked up every shirt and piece of underwear with his two fingers, shaking it and dropping on the table.

"Khmelnitsky? "Mister" Khmelnitsky, is it what you are now? Hm ... Name is ringing in my head. Wasn't it Ataman[1] Bogdan Khmelnitsky with his Cossacks chasing pretty virgins in your Stettles[2] in medieval times? Well, you are not old enough to remember that."

"Look at your round face, pug nose, and slanted Mongolian eyes in the mirror, dirty drunk," I was thinking. "Who chased your great grandmothers in time of Ghengis Khan invasion?" "Thinking" was the only thing I could do. I could hardly afford to live at this moment by my Hebrew name: "Isra-EL, the one who strives with the God." I glanced at my well-wishers warning me. "Please don't," I read in their eyes.

"Credit to your classic education, comrade officer," squeezed I through my teeth, trying not to reveal how much I 'loved' this fat pig. "My name is Khmelinsky, Jay Khmelinsky. And I love to read history books. But our plane is leaving in a couple minutes, as you know. Don't make us stay here for another day. My daughter is pregnant, and my son-in-law is squirming from a bleeding ulcer."

"Nichevo[33]," the officer said with confidence. He stepped on the shirt and sweater, the products of my full day in the store lines. He spitted on the floor through his teeth and didn't miss the sweater. "I beg your pardon, sir. Did I step on your shirt?" he said in a well-rehearsed English—the sentence, surely, he exercised by heart. The officer turned his back, signaling that he was done with "this" one.

It was no time to check the luggage. I dumped my stuff back into the suitcases like dirty garbage and dragged them toward the gate along the cardboard walled corridor, seemingly in perpetual repair. My kids were not in a position to help, and magic wheels for suitcases were still to be invented. I remembered shouting: "Don't close the doors." Or maybe I just thought I did. "Have I waved my final good-bye to everyone behind the barrier? Don't think so," blinked my mind. "I had no hands available."

I promised my mother and father to see them in less than a year.

"Never make promises you can't fulfill. It's good that I asked my uncle to stay with them for a few days," I thought. It felt as if I was attending my own funeral.

" ... Where am I going to put your suitcases now, my dear?" In the eyes of a neat flight attendant of Austrian Air I could read not just a dilemma she faced with my luggage—it was a glimmer of compassion, the sight of human face I missed so much in a course of these months of the *process*. If I had it in me at that moment, I would burst into tears and embarrass myself in front of all these people waiting for the last passenger.

I plumped into the first available chair, my shirt soaked through. Sweat streaming from my forehead wouldn't let me see a running back tarmac. But I suddenly felt my heart sink in response to takeoff. "I am free! I am flying! But I can't even lift my numb wings!" Or maybe I just thought I couldn't.

For years I was trying to join groups of tourists to some Russian satellite countries like Hungary or Poland. In the application I had to show my father's occupation. Father owned a tiny one-man photo studio in Moscow after serving four years on the front line in WWII. This "business" supported our one-room apartment for four in a Moscow suburb. Father's Red Star and Bravery medals did not prevent him from being a "blood sucking capitalist" in the eyes of authorities. So, automatically, was his son as well. And of course, my ethnicity was printed on my passport in bold letters on an infamous "Fifth Line"—the ironic manifestation of communist international solidarity. So I was rejected. And now I was flying the "Austrian Air" ... to Vienna! Not a lousy "Aeroflot" with stinky chairs and dirty bathrooms. I must have startled my neighbor when I choked on this thought.

"Bye-bye, Bear," I thought, my brain numb with excitement. "Forgive me that I gave you, the warm and fuzzy one, the same name as this horrible grizzly, called 'Communism with Human Face.' I knew, officer, what you were thinking while messing up my stuff. You were thinking about those *ghid parkhatiy*[44] leaving sinking ship for a 'glitzy' life. I have heard this so many times. I don't know how much of a 'glitz' we can buy for one hundred and twenty-five dollars of family allowance for currency exchange. But I swore to make darn sure that I would always pay my debt to my new country—whichever place it would be. I would also convince everyone to read and remember history as the best teacher one can find. Without this teacher, even direct victims of persecutions and humiliation would never admit to who they were in the hands of "merciful and misguided soldiers" of the system. They would even forget that their mothers and fathers, uncles or cousins were exterminated in some obscure places of Siberia. And please, never expect any memory from this custom officer, "the best friend of mine." People like this officer have created and fostered that grizzly of "humanity,"and they are destined now to enjoy its decaying breath. Not me! Not any more!"

... Half of my life was quickly accelerating into the past outside the round windows. The "hudge-patch" of small country izbas[55] and stand-alone suburban gardens—pride and shackles of nature loving city dwellers—were slowly fading away.

I reached into my pocket and opened a palm-sized notebook—the soaked-in-sweat witness of our ordeal. I promised myself to never put it too far away from the pencil. Well, it would come out not so easily in the busy adaptation time that was waiting for us.

chapter 2

It was 1933, time of big famine in Russia, imposed by the "brilliant" Stalin's idea of Collectivization, meaning complete and thorough anti-privatization. The only way to implement this idea was to eliminate independent farmers—kulaks—of the heavily agrarian Russia; to erase them as a class and literally exterminate the entire restless, hard working and productive group of Russian population, proud of feeding the whole world for centuries. In accordance with dogma, this "capitalistic" class should have been replaced with "politically correct and enthusiastic" agrarian lumpenproletariat, working on gigantic collective farm-factories. Siberia was the perfect instrument of extermination; vodka and propaganda—reliable tools of Collectivization and dehumanization. To make things easier, kulaks had to be sent to Siberia with their families and possessions, all the way there by foot. Weaklings wouldn't make it; the severely infirmed rest would freeze to death upon arrival. The idea was implemented by Joseph Stalin—major henchman, bank robber and, finally, the "God Father" of

Communist Mafia—with brilliant executive and propagandistic skill. Nobody was there to object.

This "procedure," by the way, was successfully repeated before as well as right after WWII on different questionable or just potentially restless groups: engineers, writers, scientists, Red Army generals, Jewish doctors, etc. That made the "Uncle Joe's" ghastly toll of extermination more than fifty million of his own citizens. This level of "success" even Hitler never contemplated. And that's not counting another thirty millions he—confused and unprepared—threw into the meat grinder of the war. What saved his butt—and the whole world, for that matter—was a historical impossibility to defeat this country of limitless resources by any conventional warfare. We do remember Goya's paintings with a horrible monster, eating his own children, don't we? Take another look.

"Oh, what about collectivization?" you may ask. Right! Well, everything was quickly "collectivized" down to the last cow in hungry peasants' homes. The peasants themselves were flocked into the collective farms like sheep and forced to work. Nobody objected. Whoever could have objected was eliminated as a "kulak"; the rest were divided in two halves. One, mostly men, was flat drunk day and night; another was subdued, submitted, and pretended to work. "Why pretend?" you may ask again. Well, the "Designer" forgot one little thing in the process—he completely forgot to provide any incentive to produce. The resulting famine—blamed of course on the "internal and foreign enemies of the state"—didn't wait for long.

• • •

My "arrival" wasn't easy. A lot of newborns in the time of famine around 1933 showed up with enlarged heads from spine inflammation called Rachitis. These heads were later commonly mistaken for ones of Socrates—even sounds similar, doesn't it? Rachitis or Socratis—who cares? Socrates probably didn't have Rachitis, and no one knows the effect of Rachitis on intelligence, but my mother often jokingly blamed me for some of her "private area" problems.

My mother was a relatively well-educated daughter of the cantor of a tiny synagogue, an incredibly mellow and wise man, the figure of my admiration. Mother spoke good Russian and had a very poetic way of writing ordinary letters. She was levelheaded and somewhat aloof. She was never strict, though. Her only way of punishment for mischief was a slight pinch of my cheek with her two fingers and a disapproving expression on her face. She was very beautiful.

At the age of five I read books by myself—a tribute to my mother. She never asked me "how" I was doing at school, but always "what." "How" was supposed to be my problem. A good source of my classic education in literature and music was radio. I could listen to David Copperfield's story over and over again, angry with that nasty flea market character, wheedling hungry David to give up his last jacket to survive. I was addicted to symphony and opera on the radio and sometimes could whistle the whole piece from the beginning to the end. Later in America, one of my colleagues, an Italian, could do the same. We improvised short competitions between our two cubicles in who could recognize the piece or whistle it more precisely. We did it pretty often for fun in the middle of the working day, to the amusement of the entire engineering floor.

My father, a photographer at the fighter plane manufacturing plant, was an affable guy with boundless drive for communication. Everyone knew Efim, and every plant worker and manager liked to have a free family picture as an official reward for good work. He was wonderful with keeping the children frozen for long exposures with the cameras of those days. He also was expert in light and composition, so the family pictures always managed to be natural and warm, the true reflection of his character. He was practically illiterate—there was no time for schooling. His big family with four brothers and two sisters was busy to repel, with the 'Maxim' machine gun in their house, the attacks of anti-Semitic bands during Civil War in Ukraine. Every time my father's family had to abandon their house under the overwhelming superiority of the enemy, they would find it intact but ransacked and used, pardon, as a comfortable outhouse. I carry the Hebrew name of one of my uncles who was killed in those skirmishes.

My brother Ned was born six years later, so I had an opportunity to usurp my father's attention and boundless love entirely to myself for six years. My father called me "My diamond." To be fair, when Ned was born, the father's treasury of diamonds doubled overnight. I saw my father's lips trembling when he talked about his sons. When I, much later, called my father from America, it was the only time I remembered him stutter. I couldn't forgive myself for not finding more time from busy life of emigration for my father, when he needed his son as much as I needed my father then. I recalled every detail of my time with the father later, after his sudden death:

- I remembered flying the training fighter plane on my father's lap—the forbidden endeavor and testimony to my father's charm, love and persistence.

• I remembered myself in the middle of the plant's soccer field during the game, hitting a rock-heavy ball with my sloppy foot and squirming from pain. "Watch your son, Efim. He could make it into our goal by mistake," joked amused players, big and powerful men I admired and envied.

• I remembered my father taking me to the old fashioned Russian public bath, a space with long stone or wooden benches and countless tin tazzas. Father would stretch me on the bench, scrub me with a loofah until every inch of my body was carrot red, and splash it with oceans of warm water. He would even take me into the steam room with big hot rocks, splashed with the water and producing clouds of white steam. There, just to give me an idea, he would whip me with birch switch for a few seconds and kick me out of the steam room.

• • •

War on our western borders didn't even start yet, but it was in full bloom in our backyards. We lived then, four of us, on a second floor of five-story building in Likhobory, on the northwestern outskirt of Moscow. We had one room in the three-room communal apartment. The room was L-shaped, making two areas almost separate. Two similar buildings formed a complex with little shallow pond in-between. This pond and adjacent area were perfect fields for contests between two armies representing Reds and Nazis. Of course nobody wanted to call himself Nazi. The common ammunitions were rocks—I wore signs of successful hits on the top of my head for long time, although as a minor I never managed to reach front line of the battle. The frozen pond was our legendary Lake Neva, where Russian Prince Alexander Nevsky, a long time ago, sank under the broken ice the heavily armored German knights with all their horses and armor. We watched that movie of Sergey Eisenstein a hundred times, supported by Sergey Prokofief's "virtual reality" music. It had the battle scenes unmatched by any filmmaker ever since. Under the night cover, just like in the movie, our backyard warriors would break the ice on the side of the peacefully sleeping enemy, in hopes that when they tried to skate in the morning, their forces would be greatly reduced. Of course, one of these holes was prepared for me, when one morning I put my skates on the woolen boots by means of ropes and sticks. I got out, breaking the ice all the way to the shores, deep in the water to my chest. My mother had lots of fun this day, applying all kind of spirits and other remedies to my body and making me sleep like a drunk. I survived.

After successful operations, our army would ambush some neighboring potato patches. We would catch a few pigeons by means of wicker baskets raised upside down on the sticks, with long rope attached to them. Meat and potato "orgy," sometimes with green tomatoes and onions, would last around the fire close to midnight, when our parents would finally raise some commotion.

When war started and real Nazis were close enough for bombing raids, life of the parents became even more stressful. Instead of hiding in the shelters, we would run up to the attic where we could see boxes with sand, extinguishers and shovels stocked against firebombs. We hoped some of these bombs would fall on our house. That would make us "firefighters and heroes." And who could miss these real life fireworks in the sky, when German planes would be crossed by the search-lights of our air defense, and the hunting would begin with thousands of guns? Then ... the splash of a precise hit, and shortly after that - the sound of an explosion on the ground with a cloud of white smock on horizon. This was an experi-ence, unmatched even close by the modern Star Wars movies and computer games.

chapter 3

Stalin has done everything in his power to undermine Russian ability to fight at the beginning of the war. He was executing every "provocateur" on the spot, which would mention Nazis as enemies after his Pact with Hitler to divide Europe. "Don't disturb the beast, and he will leave us alone," was his monumental delusion. Obviously these two systems, despite their similarity in purpose and methods, couldn't coexist. They interfered with each other in aspiration to brutalize and dominate the world. Long before Einstein came out with his theories, the Russian mathematician Lobachevsky suggested that perfectly parallel lines would inevitably collide in space due to a space non-linearity. Fascism and Communism were two parallel lines in a complex space—one on the right, another on the left—with the same mad and evil agendas.

The time for Hitler to strike seemed to be perfect. Stalin, in relatively short time of his reign, starved his population by the elimination of private farming; undermined the industrial base by extermination of best engineers and scientists;

executed his most talented generals as spies; killed every liberal leader of early Revolution as potential political rival; and oppressed the general population, particularly large minorities like Ukrainians and Byelorussians. At the beginning of invasion, Joseph Stalin, this "Eagle with Iron Wings," dropped from the scene for more than a week, trembling like a wet dog. And this was a time when disoriented Red Army, unprepared and overcome by the Nazi war machine on the western border, desperately needed guidance and was massacred, surrounded and sent to the camps by hundreds of thousands. Saddam in his "dust hole" looked the same many years later. History always repeats itself, right?

In this situation, Hitler had no doubts that Russia would fall into his hands like an over-ripened apple. The pinhead, a monster with the brain of a bird, he probably never opened the history book, the best remedy against fatal mistakes. He didn't know anything about Napoleon's ordeal in the 1812 frozen fields of Russia. He knew nothing about Peter and Catherine the Greats' expansion of Russian space and resources, making Russia unbeatable in conventional war. How would he know that Russians, when they get angry, can endure and survive more than the impossible? To throw his body on the barrel of the Nazi's machine gun spilling bullets from the bunkers was common for a Russian soldier. The first thing Hitler did at the beginning of the war—he angered this Bear. He made Russians, Ukrainians, and many others even angrier with him than with Stalin. The outcome from that point on couldn't be more predictable. It was just matter of time and price for Russia and her Allies to prevail. Hitler's ignorance in history and his monumental arrogance saved our civilization.

. . .

We could now hear German cannonade only ten to fifteen miles away from Moscow. Father's plant was still producing fighter planes, sending them to the front right from the plant's runway. The prospect to "greet" Nazi's SS exterminators was not too appealing. We were sitting on our bags, ready to go somewhere. Finally the order was given to dismantle the plant and set it up in the Central Siberian town of Omsk.

It was a two-month trip in cattle cars. For kids it was like camping in the middle of December. The evacuees waved to every stocky Siberian soldier—Sibiryak—and to every passing tank and cannon going in the opposite direction. Their priority in movement was not under dispute. Sounds of cannonade long faded away.

In my early boyhood I hated vegetable soup. Mother gave up even offering it to me any more. One day on our trip, a couple of women sitting on the edge of the cattle car's open door and eating borsch, caught me watching them with an open mouth. I was hungry. "Want some?" they asked me. This was a pleasant discovery. Borsch from that point on was my favorite dish.

Omsk was a sleepy town covered with snow to the roofs of little izbas, furnished properly by the window shutters with steel cross bars and bolts coming through the wall into the house—prudent safety measures against snow storms and burglary. Residents were allowed to keep one milk cow or a couple of goats in this time hunger, and they kept them in the house.

My grandfather, grandmother, and my uncle—the mother's youngest brother—came with us. My father and uncle were immediately mobilized and, after short training, sent to the front to join Sibiryaks. Father spent training time in a bent-in-half position, suffering from an ulcer. Later he joked that the front line was the best remedy for this illness. Father told me that he started as a front line photographer and then was advanced to the capacity of "yazyka hunter." He was now a member of the squad, sneaking, usually under the cover of the night, to the enemy position to snatch German soldier, or better an officer. This was a common tactical reconnaissance operation—satellites and "u-2s," of course, were not invented yet.

Mother replaced my father as a plant photographer. Ned and I lived with mother in a little corner of the photography studio. I quickly learned some basics of document photography and was after that an invaluable substitute to my mother and later to my father, when it was necessary.

We were hungry almost all the time, except for rare moments when some local resident would bring a chunk of butter or cheese from the produce of his cow as payment for the photo to send to the front. One commodity was relatively available, though. It was cod liver oil. Mother forced us to consume it by the spoon and fried potato in it. It was not bad, except we had to clamp our noses in a consumption process. I was nine years old and in charge of materializing ration cards at the plant store. The "ketch" was normally pretty meager. But when I was pick-pocketed a couple of times, the family really had to "enjoy" the soup made of dandelions, poison ivy and other weeds. A slice of bread with the paper- thin layer of butter was a real feast.

Once we had a nice break, though. For about one school year we got lucky—my third grade classmate, who was slightly hyperactive spoiled son of the grain warehouse director, needed some guidance and an example of a good boy's behavior. We would play together, do homework, and have a nice lunch with some doggy bag stuff sent for Ned—this family didn't have to try the weed soup.

But a real bright spot in my life was a summertime Lenin's Pioneer camp in a thick pine forest—Tayga—on the banks of Irtysh River. More regimented, it was similar to American Boy Scout camps. For about five weeks, the pioneers wore red ties, played militaristic games of Reds-and-Nazis, where Reds were always winning. We made long hiking tours through Tayga with bonfires, and swam in icy cold fast running Irtysh. I was pretty good in playing chess without a board. During the naptime, I played with one of my friends, proud of violating strict rules.

Father came back to Moscow at the end of the war homeless. Our apartment was given to somebody else with all our stuff and furniture—for the sake of "anti-privatization," of course. The tiny log cabin, we built thirty miles from Moscow right before the war and used just for few days in June 1941, was happily taken apart by the neighbors for firewood. All land, according to strict doctrine of Communism, was owned by the state. So, everything we ever had, vanished into a huge sinkhole. Father worked in his little dog-house-like studio and couldn't afford anything for his family to get together.

chapter 4

Times after the war did not match the exuberance of the glorious winners. Red Army soldiers had caught a glimpse of the Western World and were therefore the dangerous elements. The prisoners were left in German camps and eventually ended up in the West, or right upon arrival home, were sent to the far East—Yakutia, Magadan, and places on the Arctic Ocean—to mine uranium, so they would contaminate only themselves but not a general population. They would die promptly from radiation, or freeze to death back to back to each other while hoping to preserve some body warmth. Aleksandr Solzhenitsyn described all of this quite vividly in his "Gulag Archipelago," based on his own experience. Hundreds of thousands of German POWs were diligently working on reconstruction in Moscow and other big cities. They didn't speak Russian and naturally couldn't do any ideological harm. Vast areas in Ural region and Siberia were dedicated for development of nuclear and other weapons of mass destruction and world domination. These areas were completely sealed, and when horrendous accidents occurred, they were "cemented" in place with all inhabitants in them.

Stalin rapidly deteriorated into a complete maniac, looking for plots under every rug. At some point, all of more or less prominent medical doctors and professors of Jewish origin were accused of conspiracy to kill Stalin by way of "sophisticated poison or vicious medical neglect." They were put on well-fabricated trials, than executed or forced to commit suicide.

Stalin's henchmen ran smearing campaigns against the Soviet cultural elite. Every prominent writer, composer or moviemaker, whispering his own voice, was stripped of the ability to go public. The world known moviemaker, Sergei Eisenstein, director of "Battleship Potemkin" and "Alexander Nevsky," showed in his last movie "Ivan the Terrible" the character of the monstrously brutal ruler, killing his sick and mentally retarded son, who was accused of descent. Eisenstein suffered a fatal heart attack during the test show at the first sign of Stalin's disapproval—the father of the Soviet People found too much of himself in this movie and got displeased before even the end of the show. One of the best composers of our time Dmitri Shostacovich was slandered for including too many of the Nazi's militaristic tunes in his world-class symphony about the siege of St. Petersburg (former Leningrad) during the war. The great Armenian composer Aram Khachaturian, the author of the world's darlings, ballets Gayaneh and Spartacus, was severely reprimanded for not being patriotic enough in one of his last operas. Songwriters feverishly exercised in glorification of "Our Victorious Leader" in fear of being thrown out in the cold.

The charm of Stalin's appeal touched some hearts of the American and European Civil Rights movement leaders and a sizable slice of American scientific, cultural and entertainment elite. Having *no clue about reality in Russia,* they craved an "experience" of the Soviet intellectuals. Some American scientists, to their demise, considered furnishing Stalin's war machine with the knowledge of nuclear power "to balance the superpowers and save the world from a capitalistic domination." But justice and the Manhattan Project got slightly ahead of the game, putting everything in perspective. Harry Truman was one of those presidents who didn't care about 'public' opinion. He put the safety of American citizens and other first things first and solved all secondary problems later; or would rather let a resilient American Constitution solve them by themselves.

Stalin's oppression was immense, and his disapproval meant death. Even his signs of disapproval looked diabolic. The way he touched his mustache or held his pipe was enough for his hit men to know what to do. He ended like a mad dog in his sealed bunker in March of 1953 with his giant German shepherd next to him, protecting his decaying body. Nobody dared to ask: "How are you doing, Iosif Vissarionovich? Would you like some *dandelion soup with poison ivy?*"

Even Stalin's dead body proved to be deadly. Moscow streets were overfilled with mourners crying: "What we are going to do now without our father?" Thousands were trampled to death between mad crowds and military trucks, trying to break through the cordons and pay their "father" and leader their last respects.

Stalin's main hit man, Lavrenty Beria, was caught red-handed, trying to usurp dangling power. He was promptly executed, and then ... the long decades of striving for power had begun

. . .

My family was waiting for almost a year after father's return and finally came back to Moscow. Ned and I slept behind the kitchen chimney of Grandfather's one-room apartment—where our parents slept we didn't even know. Then we fostered the little daughter of an incarcerated criminal for the right to live in his apartment. We rented whatever was possible and ended up in our own one hundred square feet room in Perovo, on the eastern outskirt of Moscow. We made a kitchen-dining-sleeping room out of terrace and were using the communal outhouse for the other needs. This was our house till 1955, when I got married, and Ned, shortly after, was recruited to the armed forces.

Anti-Semitic hysteria was approaching one of its peaks. Doctors were executed—this "solved" the country's medical problems. It was a rare day when nobody mentioned my Semitic nose, called *Rubilnik* by the inventive Russian Aryans, which meant in short–the large handle of the manual electric line breaker. When it was safe enough, I replied with historic facts of Mongolian invasion and its influence on the purity of Russian race, though I wasn't sure the assailants knew what I was talking about. On one occasion in junior high school, I wasn't careful enough to quarrel with my classmate. We set up the fist duel in the school's backyard. During the fight, I was even more stupid to prevail and ended up with broken nose—the Aryan crowd of spectators couldn't stand the defeat of their brother. My "best" friend and neighbor Vasily, also a native, wiped my nose, shaking his head: "What could I do, Jay?"

I started high school in the fall of our move to Perovo. The school was located on the Highway of Enthusiasts, the long road to Siberia, used by Czarist's regime to send the old times Russian revolutionaries—the Enthusiasts—for a long walk. The same road was used for the "enemies of the state" in the modern times. But nobody called them "Enthusiasts," and even talking about that subject was not highly recommended.

The principal of my high school, the teacher of Russian language and literature, Olga Mikhailovna, was the never-smiling stately women with a noisy, ugly little dog. She walked her dog in the school garden, tended by the students for the credit in extra-curricular activity, and never let anyone enjoy it. Her arrogant attitude toward a couple Jewish teachers was monumental and very much up to the official task of the day. The teacher of mathematics, a former refugee from Poland, Mikhail Lvovich Blumencranz, was a quiet and caring man, dedicated to his profession. He spent countless hours with students who needed some help. Olga would visit his class for evaluation and publicly humiliate him. "Don't speak nonsense, Mikhail Lvovich," she would shout across the classroom.

My interaction with Olga Mikhailovna wasn't any more pleasant. One day in the class of Russian literature I had an assignment to talk about Pier Besukhov, the liberal aristocrat from the Tolstoy's "War and Piece." At this time—and not only at this one—everything made in Russia was considered to be superior to a "decadent" Western World. So I stated carefully that Pier's parents sent him to study abroad because "they considered a Russian education not good enough for their son."

"Ha," exclaimed Olga. "Are you saying that Russian education was not good enough? Khmelinsky, you are a *Cosmopolite.*"

This name in the Soviet adult world of the day was synonym of someone looking abroad and betraying his country. So, I had to be punished. In every grade of my school, beginning from the first grade, I had straight "A's" and was an obvious candidate for a Gold Medal, the open door to a majority of prestigious schools of higher education. Olga killed my medal aspirations by giving me "B's" in my Russian study and Russian literature final exams.

On the social front, however, it was an interesting time. The education was gender-separate. My classmates did not think about ethnic differences too much. We had common enemies—gangsters in the huge Ismaylovo Park and the competitors from the other boys' schools. When we were invited to a distant girls' school for dancing, we had to be vigilant. Rocks of our boyhood were replaced this time by the belts with large navy buckles. Later some, including myself, attended a class of SAMBO—the Russian abbreviation of "Self Defense Without Weapon." This kind of wrestling combined different elements of martial arts, even very offensive and dangerous ones. It was actually designed by our trainer, who spent some time in Japan. He was known also as a coach of the KGB operatives. I did not exercise this barbarian sport for too long. I rather preferred chess, swimming, volleyball, soccer, ping-pong, hockey, and cross-country skiing in Ismaylovo Park, though nowhere with "Olympic" results. Some useful elements of SAMBO, however, remained as automatic reflexes for quite an extended time. One of them, the falling-and-rolling reflex, has helped me so far (fingers crossed) to avoid broken bones in tennis. During one of my encounters with a burley anti-Semite in Ismaylovo Park, my simple 'kick-the-shin' reflex came before my brain processed the thought of possible consequences. Luckily I was wearing heavy hiking boots. This guy was disabled. Dusk and thick forest helped me to shake off the gang of his friends.

It was time for me to think about higher education. Mikhail Lvovich used to send me to a couple mathematical and physical Olympiads at Moscow University. I found myself no match to Einstein, i.e., not good enough to exploit this highly classified, and therefore, too politically and racially restricted academic field. As a Jew—potential Cosmopolite—I had to be much closer to a famous physicist in my academic abilities (the system couldn't completely close the doors to super talents without the risk of losing competitive standoff with the West for good). So, Engineering sounded much more reasonable. I sent my application for Mechanical Engineering at the Moscow Institute of Energy. As I learned, this also was *a little* too ambitious.

The Russian system of entrance evaluation was then vastly different from the American. Objective criteria did not exist. The examiner would let you take your questionnaire ticket randomly, but then he would conduct the examination in the form of an interview. He would be the only judge of the general quality of your answers and confidence. He was free to encourage or intimidate you. For one reason or another, he could help you or ask additional questions, sometimes the kind you would never be able to answer. In addition, any appeal was made impossible. I was examined side by side with an aspirant of more favorable ethnicity. I got seventeen points out of twenty, two points more than my Aryan neighbor. My mate was accepted; I was rejected.

With my score on hand, I was allowed to take correspondence courses at the Institute of Railroad Industry. I passed exams for the first year with straight "A's" and was accepted full time by the Moscow Automobile Service Institute.

This "academic" field of auto service was unique for the Soviet environment. It was invented specifically for Russian cars of a lousy quality just to keep them running. It was as important as rocket science for space exploration. Theories of the broken car's salvation were flying all over the institute's new fancy building on the Leningrad Highway. I wasn't inspired by this field of science, and a professor of the Engine Department, Tim Rozental—a tall skinny guy with my facial profile and Einstein's hair cut—helped me concentrate on design engineering. With his reference I worked on my diploma project at the Research Institute of Automobile Industry.

The fashionable ideas of automotive application of the gas turbine engine were then in the air. I was exploited there as a "demolition test bed" for the Institute's designers. Some experts in aircraft jet engines were also invited for the demolition. I would put my layouts on the board and let them be torn down piece by piece. At least they all knew now how not to design things. In order to survive, I had to plunge into a field of gas dynamics, the discipline never taught for automobile engine, which followed scientific lows of thermodynamics. It was pleasant and difficult challenge, but I enjoyed it and completed my project. My diploma presentation earned a lot of attention and drew a large crowd. It was accepted with an ovation and the highest mark. But when I asked Professor Rozental to recommend me for employment at the institute where I worked for six months on my diploma, Tim said: "Sorry, I have done for you all I could. You have to look for something less ambitious."

Recalling my diploma presentation, I sometimes suspect that there might have been another reason for its success. I was a stutterer for as long as I can remember. The legend was that sometime when I was around the age of five, my babysitter tried to control my hyperactivity by telling me a story about a wolf that ate naughty children. This super efficient pedagogic experiment coincided with the beginning of my stuttering. Whether there was any correlation or not I don't know. But at the point of stress my stuttering was so bad, I sometimes had to take oral exams in writing, in the elementary and middle school years. In my college years my problem subsided somewhat, but I was always angry that I couldn't fully express myself. With my diploma presentation, I decided to beat the "devil" at any cost. I learned that the famous Greek orator Demosthenes had a stutter. He noticed that his problem subsided when he had to over-shout the unfriendly crowd. He would go on the seashore during the surf and practice speaking, sometimes not even hearing his own voice. "What if I learn something from history?" said I to myself. I didn't expect an unfriendly crowd, and there was no sea surf in continental Moscow. But I could create noise; nobody would hear but me. Cell phones were not even in anybody's wild imagination. But I could design the noise generator, based on a regular payphone ear module; supply it with an AC current from the wall plug; hang it on my neck, and connect it to my ears by a stethoscope. It would look weird, but maybe even intriguing. The project was implemented. I couldn't hear a word of my speech, but one of my friends who participated in this experiment told me that I didn't stumble a single time. During my diploma presentation I shocked the crowd with long electric cable following me on the podium. I had to explain that it was not for communication with some clandestine helper hidden somewhere behind the scene. I think sometimes, that I wouldn't have to work so hard on my diploma, if I had come up with this idea a few months earlier—just kidding.

This experiment didn't solve my long-term problem. I attended class of autogenic relaxation. It was a technique similar to meditation, but it trained instant relaxation. This helped, but real relief came in America. Two factors worked for me in combination with relaxation: First, English is so smooth in comparison to Russian, and particularly to German, with which I had the toughest time. Second, I had to speak slowly due to my level of language proficiency, instead of jumping ahead of myself. I am doing fine now, unless I am discussing world problems with somebody of heavy socialist slant.

We were a triad of the smart-ass overachievers in our college class during periodic examinations: Averbach, Neustroev and I. Straight "A's" guaranteed a "high" stipend of fifty rubles a month, the money I needed for my books, lunches, and transportation. The college rules allowed one re-examination. We would ask the professor from the less complicated course to examine us earlier, so we would have more time for preparation or even a chance for re-examination of a more complicated course.

The strategy worked. The department secretary who prepared our diplomas told me later that she committed perjury with my diploma. She substituted a lonely "B" for an "A" in its grade attachment.

"Jay, I just didn't want to spoil it," she said sheepishly.

My daughter Lora was just born, and she managed it right on time. According to the general rules of the Russian "free education" society, the graduate had to accept mandatory work assignment—virtual serfdom—to any part of the country for three years, to fulfill his "civil" duty, and thereby pay off his free education. The families with newborn children were granted an exception. Lora was smart enough to beat the system, even at the age below zero. My career could have turned in direction I would hate all my life. So instead, I was free to go anywhere I wished.

I got job in a manufacturing support department at a tiny plant making the helicopters' props. Propellers were made out of wood and laminated in particular shape. They were covered with multiple layers of steel mesh, staples, nylon cloth, and celluloid glue. My task was to design and apply pneumatic tools, making this manual operation easier.

Celluloid, when scraped into a dust, was like gunpowder. So the fire fighting personnel were quite vigilant. They told everyone the story about how the guards, trying one day to start a stove fire with this dust and leaving box full of dust at the door, were trapped and burned alive.

One peculiar "cultural" activity, far from being limited to our plant, would be interesting to mention. It was a "civil obligation" of the employees in our department and beyond to make an excursion to the local bar on every payday—two times a month—to celebrate an ancient Russian tradition. Please don't think it was about music, dancing, nice food, or intellectual association. It was about passing down a bottle of vodka for two, and sweetening it with a piece of pickled fish or half sour cucumber. Anyone who refused to do that was considered "unfriendly and unreliable." One of our engineers, who had all the facial features of an alcoholic but hated vodka with a passion, made up a story that he was "seeded." This meant that he had a medication implant given only to the bitter alcoholics—it made vodka taste like a cod liver oil. He got an "exception" and the "hero's" regards as a staunch fighter for the *good* Russian tradition. He was my friend and shared his trick with me. I loved it, but it was absolutely inapplicable to the person of my *profile*.

During my college years, I used to utilize my long rides in the tram and subway by solving geometric, kinematic, and design homework problems. I did it the paper-less way, just like with chess in my boyhood. Working for my plant obviously wasn't one of those highly stimulating experiences. I was looking for something else. The opportunity came out. I got job at ENIMS—Moscow Experimental Institute of Machine Tools—to work in a "baby" field of machines with direct computer control. This was a leap right into a field of *high technology*.

chapter 5

The young family life doesn't normally need any essay about political background, unless, of course, this family is a "bee nest of state enemies" and a candidate for a long walk on the Highway of Enthusiasts.

Well, nobody from my family or from the family of my future wife Lena was ever involved in any political activity against the socialist state. But in some sense and at some point we in accordance with official ideological definition were qualified as "untrustworthy" or even "undesirables." For example, if I were an adult at the time I was labeled as "Cosmopolite," this could be enough for me to start gathering my bag for a long travel to the distant places. My father, before WWII as a factory worker and during the War as a soldier—unless captured alive as a prisoner of war—was qualified as "reliable." But after the war, his little "shoe polishing" size business qualified him as "untrustworthy." That's why I couldn't travel abroad, even to the satellite states.

Lena's family, however, belonged to a category of "undesirables." Her grandfather was Cantonist, Jewish boy, the servant to the army officer. As an adult, he was allowed to serve in Russian army as a soldier for twenty-five years, and only after that he got a permit to settle out of the ghetto in the "Aryan" city of Rostov. Up until the October Revolution, he was an owner of a small department store, but he lost everything during the Revolution. Lena's father tried to follow his father's path, though on a much smaller scale, after the Revolution. He spent fifteen years in Siberia in exile as a result. He came home in 1953, after Stalin's death, just to die in a few months. He was lucky not to be accused of "political incorrectness, harmful political activity," or something like that. This would qualify him as an "enemy of the state," with immediate dire consequences for him and the whole family. The entrepreneurial spirit, however, was in a genetic code of this family, and a good number of Lena's relatives paid for that.

You may ask what I think when I encounter someone craving Communism here in the West. I am trying to be as gentle as I can, holding my puke-bag available. But one question always comes to my mind: "What is it on his mind—the ignorance of an uninformed, craving for the power over the ignorant followers, or ... something much worse?" Sorry ... I promised to trust my material and keep my emotions at bay.

I got married in 1955 in the middle of my college years. Lena was a strong-willed girl with blond braids the size of baseball bat and a stubborn independent spirit. We were in love and left alone for the year before our wedding—scholarly nature of a shy Jewish boy, in Mom's opinion, warranted good behavior. So, soon I became part of a strong extended family with a powerful and spirited matriarch—my mother-in-law, who helped anyone any way she could and demanded complete submission as a pay-off. As compensation for the loss of freedom and innocence, I could now live in a part of a relatively sophisticated suburban house with the garden of about twenty-five bushes of blackcurrant, patches of tomatoes and strawberries, and some fruit trees. This allowed our family to preserve a decent amount of stuff for the winter use.

The process of preservation required some skill and even knowledge of zoology and animal behavior. On one occasion we made a foot-tall jar of half-ripe pickled cherry tomatoes. We didn't close it with a tin lid. Instead, we put clear plastic and a rubber band around it and placed the jar in the cellar under the kitchen—bad mistake! When everybody, including excited guests, was ready to try pickled tomatoes, I crawled to the cellar and found a seal broken and the jar empty. There was only some liquid and the slivers of tomato skins at the bottom of the jar. How in heaven could these nasty but apparently pretty smart house rodents manage to take tomatoes from a foot-deep jar without becoming pickled by themselves?

House still didn't have running water or bathrooms, but the makeshift heating system with registers in the kitchen stove and under every window worked perfectly. Only later, when Khruschev came out with the idea of covering Russia with the slum quality prefabricated apartment buildings "to provide an apartment for every Soviet citizen" was our house demolished. We moved into a two-bedroom apartment on the second floor of a five-story building.

Our wedding was a most unforgettable event. I couldn't allow myself to be grossly outnumbered by this large family of assertive relatives and friends, so I demanded a parity. I invited an equal number of my relatives—many of them I had seen not more than once in my life. The wedding was fun. Guests sat on each other's laps like herring in the can, enjoyed wonderful food, which my mother-in-law could prepare in a moment with one arm tied behind her back—just to be fair to the general populous. The reception ended way after midnight. I parted with my friends ... and never saw many of them again.

I wouldn't call my family a "Mecca of prosperity" by any means: I was heavily relying on my stipend and did some photo-touch work for my father. We were doing lots of work in our house for a local textile plant. Our young family vacations were not exactly Caribbean "Celebrity" adventures. We would often paddle down the river or across the lakes in a large foldable kayak. We fished and swam somewhere in pristine places. The only problem was: the kayak added a couple of heavy pieces of luggage to be transported to and from the bus or train to the place of launch. On top of everything, we had to carry a complete supply of canned food for the whole vacation. On one occasion I was disabled for a good part of our vacation after I moved around all of this stuff under the flu condition; on the other we ran out of food, stopped at the country store and found the store shelves full of ... nothing but vodka. You are laughing, aren't you? We did not. We were in a precarious situation with no way to buy *any* food. We finished our vacation on old shrunk potatoes, and whatever fish we could catch. How could ordinary Russians survive in places like this, is a very good question.

In 1957, our daughter Lora was born after I came home from extended military training, hungry not only for the food. Lora became the mother-in-law's monumental life-long obsession. Fortunately, Lena was on my side, helping me to avoid a child-fostering disaster. Noone knows how, but we had made it. I've now got with me in America one smart, beautiful and caring daughter, the delight of everyone she manages to touch with her spirit. During the difficult emigration and adaptation period, we were not always in tune with each other's needs. We got a heartwarming chance to catch up years later. One of the problems, though, of living apart is a mounting phone bill when we debate our philosophical differences. She is a rock-solid New Englander—what can you do?

When we moved into an apartment, Lora was a baby. We made a healthy but, as I can think now, a pretty brave habit. We would leave her on the balcony in a stroller for the daytime nap, even in the winter under almost any weather. The number of blankets applied was calculated "scientifically" upon outside temperature. Another healthy factor Lora grew up with came a few years later. One day I returned from a business trip, opened the door of our apartment, and was greeted by the good sized black, furry ball joyfully jumping right on my chest. I almost fell downstairs. It was a standard poodle, still a puppy, big enough to knock you off your feet.

"What do you think?" Lena asked. "I got her from my friend, who was going away for a long time and couldn't keep her."

Terry has become a long time joy of our family, Lora's best friend, and an entertainer for the entire neighborhood. Terry's playful character and fire-like temperament were of a boundless love. There was no way for anybody to play soccer, volleyball, or basketball when Terry was around. The players would stop their games; form the big circle, with Terry in the middle, trying to catch the ball. She would jump six feet high, turning and flipping like in a circus. I have a picture of her jumping over the four-foot fence with her legs and body forming a straight arrow. She would do that and other tricks fearlessly over and over again. She was kidnapped a couple times for ransom—she wasn't afraid to come to anyone and had no concept of danger. When we emigrated, we left her with Lena. Terry lived with her till about eighteen years old—the human age equivalent of one hundred. She was still slender and beautiful and was stolen again—blind, deaf, and partially gray. I had few dogs in my life. The only dog comparable somewhat with Terry was a tiny five-pound toy poodle named Apry, who has been my walking buddy. He is six now, well behaved, and full of love for everyone he sees. I have read about a poodle's territorial instinct. Maybe poodles keep it to themselves, but I had poodles of all sizes in a course of my life, and none of them ever barked to protect their territory. Their snobbish response to noisy dogs had always been: "You can bark, I don't care. I won't even look at you, noisy creature." Or maybe they just reflected their master's character? . . . Just kidding again. Some of Apry's famous circus tricks have been ringing the bell when asking for the treat, and shaking his collar tags when asking to go out.

People ask sometimes why the state of Israel is so overpopulated with musicians—as Vienna with poodles, by the way. The answer, I guess, is simple: If native Russians spent all the money and effort, they wasted on vodka, just to give their children the joy of music, Russia would also be overpopulated with musicians—the Russian genetic code, as history shows, is not at all foreign to music. Then maybe as a nice side effect, the whole course of our civilization would be much more pleasant. Following this motto, we pushed a vocational music education down Lora's little throat. She even graduated from the school of Children's Music Education. She didn't become another Bella Davidivich by any means, but she passed musical tradition to her children and didn't mind possessing some musical background herself, just for the fun of it.

We were basically a "alright" couple during our marriage. But at some point the differences in characters and values took their toll. I've always been an introvert and individualist, seeing my joy in creative work. Lena is the outgoing, giving and demanding champion type of personality, just like her parents. We started to drift apart. And when I suggested emigration, she said: "I don't think you are going to make it in this harsh, capitalistic world." This had solved our marriage dilemma. Unlike Lena, I had reason to believe that marketing and sales were not the only professions respected in the American economy. And with my lifestyle, I didn't need much material wealth to be happy—just a little love and an understanding. To my delight, Lora decided for herself, and Lena had enough common sense not to resist. Lora is happy that I've been maintaining friendly and respectful relationship with her mother, who is still quite a character, and I admit, a pretty successful businesswoman. After all, marriage is just a volunteer union of two intelligent people, or at least it's supposed to be, isn't it?

chapter 6

The Soviet Empire was entering its final stage. Stalin's successors were replacing each other at a dazzling speed, with the same flat faces coming back and forth. Neither of them had any idea how to hold this rotting giant intact—economically, politically, morally, or in any other sense.

They poured huge resources into *pokazuha*,[67] trying to convince the West and their own satellites in the viability of the System. Sophisticated facilities were erected and subsidized to develop and show to the West some modern models of Soviet technology. Nobody in the industry was interested in its honest use, though—the old ways in the environment of no competition were much easier: "Why bother if a lousy product of the only factory around can be snatched by the hungry consumer in a split second?" But on paper, of course, everything was going "hunky-dory." The paper would tolerate anything, as Stalin himself once cynically remarked.

Satellite countries were becoming restless. To control their behavior, the empire reserved to all kinds and means of intimidation. Hungary and Czechoslovakia tasted hot metal of Russian guns and tanks. East Germany was covered with a cloud of medieval inquisition and surrounded by a thick concrete wall.

Khruschev, in the mean time, was banging the UN table with his shoe and promising to beat the West to submission with the power of the Soviet economy. His escapades were met as a joke of a very bad comedian. In Russia, Khruschev was universally regarded as a jerk. His illiterate attempts to articulate the impossible were subject of countless anecdotes on the streets and in living rooms. Everyone knew the value of speeches at work and public forums. The same speaker was expected to be honest when he was off the podium and surrounded by a small group of intelligent people. Here he would receive a friendly pat on the shoulder: "Come on, pal, cut out your bull crap."

Soviets needed help from the West they pledged to kill. The policy of denying Soviet Jews the right to join their families, dispersed all over the world by the Nazi's Holocaust, didn't look very appealing. To stop the Exodus, Soviet tacticians imposed huge "redemption fees" on professionals as a compensation for free education—they forgot for a moment that these professionals had already paid their dues through the years of slave labor. The Western Jewish community responded instantly: "We will pay. Let them go!"

Then the authorities came out with a *brilliant* solution. They would randomly select scapegoats, declare them "in possession of state secrets," and intimidate the rest of the potential applicants. People, quite naturally, would be restrained by gloomy prospects of becoming outcasts forever, for no reason and with no explanation. They would have no jobs and no means of living. Possession of all material means by the state in the totalitarian environment was total and absolute. That's probably why this ideology was officially called in every schoolbook: "The Marxist-Leninist Dialectic Materialism." Who would prove the validity of accusations in possession of state secrets? They were the secrets in the first place. "It's not our fault—see, people don't like to leave their Motherland," the Soviet propaganda would say with "innocent" wonder. The communist idea of absolute government control of material assets and people's lives worked wonders for almost seventy years.

Well ... not anymore. Time was getting ripe for Valensa, Pope John-Paul II, Reagan and Gorbachev.

...

A job at ENIMS was a perfect heaven of perpetual education at the government's expense, and a living example of "viability and vitality" of the Soviet economy. I started in 1960 at the newly formed Department of Computer Controlled Machine Tools.

It was common for the people then to ask: "Why bother with these complicated and unreliable gadgets if we can get the country women (men were too busy drinking) to do this job for five rubles a day?" But policy makers and the grassroots of engineering curiosity prevailed. The systems, developed in the lab, did not see much of a real life production, but they drew the attention of retired tourists from American towns and other similar places. When something in the system functionality was subject to worry, we would hide someone close by with the "emergency" button in his hands to reactivate machine, stuck in a maze of high technology.

In 1965 I was transferred to the Department of Dimensional Metrology. This field suited me particularly well, due to my perfectionist nature. I had to deal with the precision geometric measurements of machine parts and the functional performance of the mechanisms, often using lasers, and later, computer controlled measuring machines. Very sophisticated Metro-Lab and optical scale production facilities were built on the third level down underground to maintain tight temperature control. Crowds of foreign dignitaries were brought to this facility from more important places. Results, however, were not any different. The effort still did not see any application. One would ask: "Why such an elaborate scheme for a zero result?" Well, in the time of Sputniks and nukes, designed for propaganda and intimidation, this was a trick to show some "balanced" nature of the Soviet economy.

Not all, however, was for nothing in my activity. Some of it in those days had real social and economic impact, both on my country and me. A few times I had an opportunity to organize groups of eight to twelve specialists from ENIMS to work deep in Siberia during our extended vacations for the sake of a thrill, companionship and extra money. On one of such projects, for example, the team would be putting together some production units for prefabricated construction parts in Tiksi City on the shores of the Arctic Ocean. In another, we tied log rafts in the middle of the fast running Angara River in the very center of the Siberian forest—Tayga. Here we would receive the 5-ton bundles of logs, dumped into the river by the tractors from the river bank, direct and sort them out afloat, and ride them to the proper point on the raft. Then we would tie them to the raft at the point where they belonged. This was more of a thrill than taming the wild mustangs in America.

After a day of work, we drank pure (100%) alcohol, common for the area; all stayed in a one-room log cabin on the slides, to be pulled by the tractors anywhere it was supposed to be; cooked on the fire; sang Russian ballads; and were eaten alive by the hungry mosquitoes, if we didn't hide ourselves under the water in the middle of the river. A stock of rubles, a healthy but slightly uneven tan, and tons of pictures and memories were decent compensation for some discomfort.

Another form of my useful supplemental activity was translation of technical literature from English and German to Russian for some industrial publications and patent bureaus—"almost" the early Einstein's type of work. This did not help much with speaking skills later on, but it was a modest moneymaker and useful professional experience. Those were my ways to survive and support my family.

But in the fall of 1976, we finally decided to let Russian industry and ideology solve their problems without our help. We applied for emigration.

Shortly before application, America herself came to Moscow to show her economic and cultural achievements. It was a display of fantastic panoramic views of New York Harbor, the Manhattan skyline, national parks and forests, and all kinds of technical gadgets. Nobody here needed any help from a hidden technician with the emergency buttons.

I met with an American guide, a Mediterranean looking guy with the round beard of Karl Marx.

"Are you going to America? Don't. America, worse than anyone else, is destroying its environment. In no time you will find yourselves in sewage with no water to drink."

I shivered for a moment from this prospect ... but then, slightly confused, told him, with the help of interpreter, about how Russians destroyed all lakes and rivers in their Middle Asian Republics already. I also told him that I had seen Lake

Baikal in the middle of Siberia. It was the deepest and used to be the biggest source of pristinely fresh water. The beautiful lake was contaminated by the cellulose production and now looked like a mud hole from the air. It used to be the lake with thousands of unique fish and other species, largely extinct now. So I ignored the advice of this strange guy, but was left with a somewhat unsettled feeling. Lots of things in the American frame of mind and political currents were yet to be sorted out.

I was lucky to avoid the iron rake of Soviet propaganda machine. The bureaucratic system fortunately failed me. The day before my application I even received a Gold Medal for one of my machines that I presented at the Moscow International Machine Tool Show. So, I was going to America as a decorated technocrat. Well, nobody cared here about my Medal. I learned that people have different values in this America, and they don't give a thought about medals minted in Russian language.

Right before an application for emigration Lora married a young man from the league of "undesirables." Bob got his stomach ulcer from multiple encounters with agencies of "Illegal Economic Activities" for trading used jeans with foreign tourists. It was a post-Khruschev's time of "Socialism with a human face," and Siberia was considered too harsh for this kind of capitalistic activity. But Bob was more than ready to get out.

chapter 7

Vienna and Rome were the international hubs of Jewish escape to the West and state of Israel. Different charitable organizations, working in these two cities, helped new refugees settle in the country of their destination. The Israeli agency SOHNUT dealt with the groups heading to Israel directly from Vienna. They would receive help, language and job training, and become citizens of the state of Israel immediately. HIAS, helping refugees of different ethnicity settle in the West, would move them in a couple weeks from Vienna to Rome, where they were receiving help and training while waiting for the visas to United States, Canada, Australia, or New Zealand. HIAS would pay freight, living and training expenses, and expected gradual reimbursement and participation in charitable affairs from the refugees after they settled. The system worked like a well-lubricated recycling machine.

. . .

Our plane was heading for a landing at the Vienna Airport. Touchdown felt very smooth. How could it be not with all our tension and anticipation? Loud applause erupted—the plane carried a sizable crowd of refugees.

My first experience in the West was in a men's room. Pristinely clean and sparkly, it was in such stark contrast with the shabby and muddy Russian toilets that I had to fight my instinctive desire to take a drink from the toilet bowl, just like that caveman lost in a civilized world. The attendant pointed his finger to the plate with coins. I apologized and promised to pay double next time when I would get some Austrian currency. My German helped. Unlike English, which I tried to learn by myself, it was my second tongue at school—I grew up in a generation of the war with Germany, as you know.

We were in the hands of SOHNUT now. The tall, red-haired representative of Israel was eloquent and persuasive. So were two Israelis, a young man and a girl, we had an interview with the next day. Beautiful people, neatly but modestly dressed, with large sparkly eyes, they made everyone feel as if we were betraying our country. A decision was already made, however. We had friends waiting for us in Rhode Island, and also some prospects for me to work in my professional field.

Cousin Minna showed up, imposing and confident, with roses for Lora. Minna and her husband Sasha had settled in Vienna, ran a small business, and helped HIAS in the refugees' interim accommodation. She rejected the advances of the flamboyant red-haired Israelite off hand and dumped on the table a mountain of yogurts in colorful plastic cans. Yogurt was delicious.

Exhausted after a few hours of waiting and confusion, we were finally placed in the little inn of Frau Bettina. She liked to joke: "We waited for you for thirty years. You can wait for a few hours." The inn was a place with small rooms, public toilets, and public bathtubs. As the newcomers learned later, it was also a place with some rooms rented by the hour. The seniors got perfect entertainment. They would sit in the inn's foyer on the bench, gossip, and watch steady streams of representatives of the oldest profession, waving their hips in super short skirts and following their men upstairs.

The next day we strolled along the neighboring streets, stopped by the little deli store, and almost fainted from the powerful scent of fresh deli. "I would charge everyone just for the smell," Bob said in amazement. "What if we asked this nice looking lady to cut a thin slice of each kind of meats and cheeses for us?" I suggested. "Would she call the police to throw us out of the store?" In Russia, this kind of request would be considered insaine—wasting valuable time of busy citizens. The lady smiled, unwrapped every block of goodies we wanted to taste, wrapped every slice separately in transparently thin paper, and put everything in a nice plastic bag. We bought a loaf of warm French bread and a big bottle of orange soda. We took it all home and had the feast of our lives. I still feel an aftertaste of this bread, cheese and salami.

The next morning was for an exploration of the farmer's market. We came across a young, scraggly looking couple, the American Maoists as we learned. The couple called Russians and Americans the "damn imperialists" and said China's was the only way to go.

"You . . . went to China?" I said in my broken English.

"We don't have to," they answered.

"Why?"

"Some bureaucrats in China, or maybe in America, screwed up our application. It's too far, anyway."

"Go, and don't come back," I said to myself.

In all other aspects, they were a pleasant and intelligent couple, amusing and entertaining.

"What's going on in their sick minds?" I wondered with bewilderment again.

We needed two weeks to complete our American visa application. In the mean time, we were busy. We borrowed some money from Minna and plunged into a sweet life. We visited the Maria Theresa National Museum of Fine Art; grandiose St. Stephen's cathedral; palaces and parks of Austrian Imperial past—Schoenbrunn and Belvedere. We enjoyed Prater—the huge amusement park with an interacting Zoo and the horror shows. We watched *Saturday Night Fever* with sexy John Travolta; walked the fashionable Koerntner Strasse with neon lights and amazing flower shops; and tried the coffee "Melange" with fantastic pastries at the bistro on the sidewalk, priced at the level of our daily allowance. We even peeked into the red-light district area, and also looked with amusement at the toy-size gardens and equally tiny recreational vehicles, which Austrian seniors maintained in the pristine way in the city and on its outskirts.

Once, on the lawn of Maria Theresa Plaza, we bumped into a recent Russian immigrant to the United States, a young medical doctor traveling in Europe. "I don't like Austria," he said. "I have bought shoes here, put them on, walked a few blocks, and got blisters. The store refused to take these shoes back. I don't believe it!"

"This man apparently has completely blocked the history of Russian experience out of his memory, as if it never existed," I thought in amazement.

We made friends with Boris, the young emigrant from Kishinev, a capital city of Moldavia, the ethnic region in the western part of Soviet Union. He was a jazz musician and had settled in Vienna. One day, Boris took us to his summerhouse in the country. His car broke down, and we didn't have time to wait for it to be fixed, so we took a bus. The house was one of those "toy" RVs, set on a toy-size piece of land. A couple dozen of similar units were situated around a tiny pond. Every yard was decorated with flowers and small bushes. Boris's yard wasn't in the best shape, and we spent the whole afternoon to take care of it. Then we had a barbecue and wonderful Viennese coffee. When we finished, it was too late for the bus. We hitchhiked for about an hour, trying to stop a car with enough space for the four of us.

"I have an idea," Boris suggested when we lost hope. "Let's use Lora as bait. We will hide in the bushes and leave our beauty on the road. When the car stops, we will ambush it and give the driver a choice: roll us over, or take us all in." The strategy worked like a charm. A first car, the full-size Ford, had stopped dead. To compensate for deceit we tried to entertain the driver with horrible stories about Siberian blizzards, bears, and the yard-long fish. Not exactly happy with our trick, he kicked us out on the outskirt of Vienna at the tram stop. He gave us lazy smile, waved his middle finger, and took off.

Contrary to Russian doctor and besides the hitchhiking episode, I found Austrians well-disciplined, reserved and polite people. They guarded their way of life and privacy, but were also willing to go out of the way if they were asked for help. On one occasion, for example, we asked a middle-aged man for directions. It was raining. The man tried to explain, but we couldn't understand him. Then he opened his umbrella and walked with us for a couple of blocks to show us the direction. Yes, in this country, traffic would stop dead if someone stepped on the road. No, the Austrians wouldn't like you to bend pages of a fresh magazine on the newsstand and put it back without buying it. It would just go against their cultural grain. Austria, now a second rate country, is living with a bouquet of issues regarding its controversial—at best—grass-root role in the Holocaust. One of the results of ethnic cleansing during WWII was complete depletion of the intellectual and scientific basis of this country, known in the past as a "brain-house" of Europe.

We were ready now to move to Italy, just over the Goddard Pass, into the world vastly different. In Italy, warm and outgoing people would hang laundry between houses, walk in the middle of the street, and block all the traffic when their soccer team won. It would also be a country where drivers would maneuver in all this mess; where young motorcyclists would snatch handbags off the careless tourists and emigrants, and victoriously run away.

Sasha dropped us at the railroad station with our entire luggage. The Vienna-Rome train was waiting at the platform, surrounded by the heavily armed Austrian National Guard. The travelers learned that last time the Palestinian terrorists ambushed this train—it was carrying some Jewish refugees. Few people were hurt. Terrorists had found an easy target. Of course, they wouldn't stand a chance to do it with Israel's El-Al Air Line heading to Palestine, though the more desirable target of terror.

It was the overnight train. Italian police replaced the Austrian ones at the stops. Suddenly, early in the morning, the train stopped in the middle of nowhere. We were ordered to get out with all our possessions and move quickly to the busses waiting for us along the railroad. A group of very serious looking men with machine guns helped us to board the buses, and the caravan took off. In an hour we were in Rome in our hotel, with the same men watching us unload. Later we learned that HIAS hired the local mafia to protect refugees. The Geneva Conventions didn't bind our guards. The terrorists, if caught, could most likely face in their hands the *medieval treatment* with the heavy flavor of inquisition. And they knew that.

We rented one room of a two-room apartment on Via Primavera, the top floor of a four-story stucco house. It was the only apartment on that level. The rest of the roof served as a huge balcony with a view of the surrounding neighborhoods. We called it "Our Solarium" and spent most of the time of our four-month stay in Rome on this balcony. The way to our apartment led through the stairs with a swarm of countless cats in possession of our landlady. Fortunately, these cats didn't show any interest in the fourth floor. I put my cot on the balcony and slept there. Sometimes the rain greeted me. The whole sky of Roman stars in the mean time was in my possession.

It was a hot summer. Roman streets were smoggy; travel to HIAS Center of Adaptation was pretty crowded, and we were exhausted. But we were determined to see as much of Rome as possible. We visited the Vatican with its endless museums and Sistine Chapel; saw a panorama of Roman Forum ruins; and attended one of the most celebrated opera concerts on its grounds—of course behind the fence, since we did not have money for the tickets. We went to the Coliseum, walked Imperial and Romantic Rome all over, and enjoyed the best panorama of the Eternal City from the steps of Garibaldi's Monument. We "witnessed" the whole tenure of the Pope John-Paul and his funeral, and "elected" the Cardinal Voitilla, as Pope John-Paul II, to lead Crusade against communism.

One late Sunday afternoon, we stumbled into a gorgeous

iron fence of the large two-story villa under restoration. The beautifully designed flower garden was in full bloom. The gates were locked. It was dusk, and there was no single light in the villa.

"Looks like nobody is around," Bob said with a conspiratorial grin. "What if we climb over the fence and take a walk in this beautiful garden."

"Are you crazy? Your wife is in her fifth month of pregnancy."

"I want to walk in this garden," cried Lora. "You will help me. Come on. Can two men help one woman?"

"We will be arrested and kicked out of Italy. It seems like some museum," I said, looking around. Nobody was in the vicinity at this corner. Decision came first, the prudence we considered when we came home excited about this crazy adventure. I quickly climbed the fence and jumped onto the lawn. Bob lifted Lora on his shoulders, and I caught her on the other side. Alone in this garden, we approached the villa and looked through the windows.

"Look, the room is crowded with vases," whispered Lora. "It *is* a museum!" As we learned later, it was National Museum of Villa Julia, the precious collection of archeological findings of Southern Etruria. Vases were the world known authentic Italian Etruschi.

"Let's get out of here," whispered Lora again.

"No, we have to wait till its dark," I said. "And I want to enjoy the fruits of our crime to the fullest and explore this garden. If they arrest us, it will be at least for something" We spent most of the evening in a fragrant fog of flowers, and went home well after midnight on the last tram.

Streets of the city were crowded with youth day and night. The Roman youth, both men and women, were an exceptionally attractive crowd, perfectly matching romantic Rome and having a wonderful time. Lots of churches were often used for all kind of musical concerts and festivals. Romans could always entertain themselves at a reasonable price. One of such concerts, which we attended in an American church, was with the famous Russian pianist Bella Davidovich.

I was running around like a hungry maniac, but Lora couldn't keep up the pace any longer, and our squad drifted apart in our tourist agendas. At some point, to the men's selfish delight, Lora had to dedicate her time mostly to culinary activity. We were amazed how much of this art could be transferred by means of genetics and a good example from one generation to another. I did not know when I would come back to Italy again, so I decided to make the Italian adventure intensive enough to last in my memory for a lifetime.

My goal wasn't easy to fulfill. Lots of precious art works of Michelangelo, Raphael, Caravaggio, and others were hidden in small and obscure churches. The churches themselves, often very modest in exterior, would suddenly open a magnificent interior, and vice versa. It was like walking on a ground made of precious gemstones, covered with centuries of dust. I lost eight to ten pounds, and my pants needed serious alterations, but I didn't care. I only regretted that so many weekdays were busy at HIAS.

Now I wanted to see Michelangelo's David in Florence, the Leaning Tower of Pisa, and the canals of Venice. I bought a second-class "kilometrico" train ticket, allowing me to use it any time at any place in Italy. I put the backpack with a sleeping bag and a load of can food and crackers on my shoulders (experience never fades), and abandoned HIAS for a week.

In Venice, I rode the canal trams, wondering how long the magnificent palaces, submerged in the water, could survive. I attended an art fair on the St. Mark's plaza and enjoyed a festival of music, dancing, youth and laughter. I slept on the steps of the railroad station with hundreds of students around, and often asked myself: "What in heaven is this forty-four years old idiot doing in the sleeping bag on the steps of the station in this crowd of youngsters?"

I had some "intellectual" debates with some youngsters on the railroad station steps. Again I wondered: "Either I am absolute moron, or the brains of these teens are heavily contaminated with lots of trash."

Heavy rain woke me up on the park lawn in Florence. It didn't matter. I found shelter in a telephone booth. In an hour, I was already surrounded and overwhelmed by Michelangelo, Leonardo, and Titian in the city of Dante. I ran all aver the place and slept in the park. I couldn't feel my legs and forgot to eat.

Then in Pisa, I was wondering how the inventive Italians were going to stop the tower from falling down. My pants now looked like an empty bag. One criminal thought crossed my mind a couple times during these adventures: "Why didn't I just buy a stack of cheap post cards with all these nice pictures to feed my soul and save my body." Well, I didn't dwell too much on it.

My last adventure in Italy was a bus trip south, arranged by an entrepreneurial group of refugees. I visited: Sorrento; seducing and dissolute Pompeii, punished for its sins; the endless 24–7 live flea market, called Naples; and little Capri, with its blue-blue shores, grottoes, and amazing rock formations in the middle of the strait.

The real emotional experience in Rome was saved for dessert, when HIAS center demonstrated the movie "Fiddler on the roof" with amazingly warm and "Jewishly" wise Topol.

I read *Sholom Aleichem* from cover to cover when he was published in Russia for the first time, at the period of "thaw" after Stalin's demise. But this was invitation to the New World, where one would never be declared an outcast by the government for political or racial reason, no matter how many wicked or stupid people would want him to be this outcast.

Our visas to Rhode Island were ready. It was time to board the enticing Boeing 747. Custom officers were polite and business-like. The flight attendants were the most beautiful girls we had ever seen. And nobody, *I mean nobody*, stepped on my new Italian shirt.

"Bye-bye, Rome! See you later, the 'Old' World. Thank you so much for your hospitality!"

chapter 8

America, as we know, has been the country of new emigrants throughout its history. These emigrants have been bringing a respect for their new country's laws and traditions, their difficult experience, vigor, enthusiasm, and incredible cultural diversity. More often than not, children would rapidly bypass their parents in English, education and cultural assimilation, and become very valuable parts of society, united in its common, positive goal. The place in which they are living and working now isn't perfect, but who could recall anyone buying a return ticket from the United States? The stream has always been like in a diode—in one direction.

Some emigrants would come alone and without any support system in place. Naturally, they would struggle the most in their adaptation. The others were lucky to have somebody waiting and caring, ready to offer a hand when it was really necessary. We were among the lucky ones.

• • •

We landed at the Kennedy Airport on August 31 at 8 PM. The outside air took our breaths away. It was hot and muggy. *Hello, New York*, I said to myself. *Are you always like that?*

HIAS was working like a clock. Documents were distributed in minutes. Porters were running with the luggage at cosmic speed. Nobody asked for tips—probably HIAS took care of it. In an hour we were in our chilly-fresh hotel room, overwhelmed and happy.

It was not too late. "Is there anything interesting to see around the hotel?" I asked the nice little lady at the counter. "We don't walk around in this area at night," she said with smile. "Why?" I insisted. "You will see in the morning, sir," she replied. It was pre-Guiliani's New York, as I learned later. And my mentality was still in Russia, where crime was either brutally repressed or swept under the rug, so nobody would know about it.

The flight to Providence, the city of our destination, took forty minutes. We saw a panorama of small residential homes completely immersed in a lush carpet of trees and embraced by the deep bay and ocean shores. A silly question crossed my mind: "Who is taking care of all this beauty?"

At the exit doors of a small and very cozy airport we were greeted by our sponsor, Oleg Sabinkin, and two representatives of the Jewish Family Service, a charitable agency that helped new refugees settle.

Oleg, my former colleague from ENIMS, took a special place in our emigration process. We both worked at the same department of metrology. Unlike me, the bookworm and lonely inventor, Oleg was a brilliant, outgoing marketer and communicator with fluent English and rare technical baggage. He was responsible for the import of foreign equipment that was required for our Metro Lab, and he also served as a real time interpreter. He was ready for the West. And when he emigrated with his wife Inna and his two boys in 1976, his job at the company, which he helped out in Russia, was waiting for him. He worked as a manager of marketing support and was the company's spokesman for over a quarter of a century. Now, in his mid-seventies, he is still working part time for the same company, and still considered to be a valuable asset.

Oleg assumed the role of sponsor for my family and me, and this carried serious responsibility. The sponsor would put his reputation in the community on the line. He would guarantee, with his honor and assets, that the person he recommended would be a valuable member and pay his dues off the first moment he could.

After twenty minutes of driving on highway, arched by lush trees, we were in the second floor apartment of a cute, small house full of people we had never seen. We were greeted by the loud welcome cheer, stunned and speechless. The apartment was equipped with modest but clean furniture, appliances, kitchen gadgets, dishes and utensils. Some of these items are still being used. The refrigerator was full with tender care. "Who put all this stuff here?" I whispered with amazement. Oleg put his arm on my shoulder and said softly, but loudly enough for everyone to hear: "Relax, your turn will come." I looked at myself in the big mirror hanging in the foyer; I looked at Lora and Bob—we almost definitely needed this big refrigerator full to the hilt.

Our first interaction with the outside world of business was not so pleasant. We needed a car, and the one hundred and twenty dollars didn't promise much. Finally we came across with a 1970 Ford Grand Torino. The seller was eloquent—the buyers were desperate. As I learned, this combination was not necessarily business-healthy. So we bought the car, and it started to leak three blocks away from the seller's home—the radiator was cooked.

The Grand Torino was a car just for me. I was a new driver and never had a car in Russia, although by my engineering degree I was supposed to be a "specialist" in car service, with a fleet of Volgas and Zims in my possession. The gas turbine engine I designed in Russia for my diploma, although "ground breaking," didn't have wheels and brakes, and wouldn't by definition move me around too far.

I had an international driving license, though. I got it as a part of mandatory college credit, driving an old WWII era truck a couple of times. During the driving test, the whole group of students would sit on the floor of the truck. They would descend in turn into the cabin next to the examiner to take a few minutes drive around the block. So, as can be seen, my experience with American highways was purely theoretical, although legally I had all rights to drive anywhere I wished. On top of that, the Grand Torino was known for its very small embrasure-like oval windows. I drove some tanks during military training in the Red Army during college. Torino was much worse. I could see only two lines, driving in the middle of my lane—never mind controlling the situation on the road.

My spoken English was even more serious cause for concern. I could translate technical literature practically without a dictionary and somehow understand the English of my teachers in Rome. But when I turned on the TV set here, I could hear nothing but an unrecognizable, mile-long word of something.

"Is this a well admired New England dialect?" I mused, looking helplessly at the screen. "I am in a deep trouble now."

But America couldn't wait too long to be "conquered."

Still in Rome, I received an invitation for an interview with Oleg's company, "The Precision Product." My interviewer, Olash Partosh, manager of engineering, was a Hungarian refugee. He did not speak good English either. If someone had recorded our conversation at the time of the interview, I would sell it to a comedian and make a hit out of it. To make long story short, Mr. Partosh didn't like my English and didn't hire me. Later, when I was working for someone else, "Precision" made desperate attempt to compete with my company on our turf. The machines I helped to develop by this time made this effort futile. As I learned from Oleg, the common joke between some funny guys at the "Precision Product" was: "Do you know why Partosh didn't hire Jay? Oh, yeah, he didn't like his English."

There was only one company left in my professional field in the region, the "Harp Manufacturing." The company was developing and manufacturing machine tools and made its fortune during WWII, producing the shell making automates. Only recently they penetrated the field of dimensional measuring machines, the area I was somewhat familiar with. Few Russians émigrés were working for this company in capacities from machinists to design engineers. They were all doing well and opened a little door of confidence for other Russians. I had nothing to lose, sent my resume … and got an interview.

Now, with the help of my "tank," I had to conquer twenty miles of highway with a couple intricate exits. Minding that my first exit would be on the left, I was driving in the left lane of the speedway, "safely" at forty-five miles per hour. I was disregarding some finger signs of the obnoxious drivers cutting me off, the signs I still knew at this point nothing about. The next thing I saw was my final exit.

"Oh, no! It can't be! Do they have multiple exits with the same names in this strange country?"

How I'd gotten there, I had no idea, but my "left-lane" strategy apparently worked. As I realized later, it may have saved my professional career.

...

The company's facility was a beautiful modern building designed by Mrs. Harp, wife of Mr. Harp, the chairman of the board. He was also the great grandson of the company's original founder. The one-story building was spread wide in a lush forest. The parking lot was crowded with cars. I didn't notice a single "tank" on this lot.

My interview was with Nick Cook, the polite and slightly gregarious manager of engineering. He was in his early fifties. I presented to him my honor diploma with famous straight "A" enclosure, the Gold Medal from the show, and a manuscript of my Ph.D. thesis, which I completed and presented to my scientific colleagues, but didn't have time and desire to formalize in Russia. Mr. Cook pushed this stuff back and said: "Thank you. I don't speak Russian. I would rather be more interested in something else."

He asked me how I would design measuring machines, and why would it be this way but not the other. Noticing my considerable struggle with non-technical part, he gently slid a notebook with a pen toward me and smiled. I was much better off with my sketches and simple formulas. The interview lasted for a couple hours. "Well, well," Nick said finally. "Interesting exchange. Thank you for your time, *Dr.* Khmelinsky. I hope to have a chance and pleasure to see you again."

On my way back, I got lost at least five times—I completely forgot about my strategy. All the way home I was thinking: "How would it look if Mr. Cook asked me about something in which I was much more competent and experienced? I would probably fail."

An offer came pretty quickly. Nick took me to the lab, pointed at the skid crowded with pieces of the company's first table top manual measuring machine, and said with a broad grin: "It's all yours, sir. Put it together and make it run. Tell me what's wrong with it, and how you would make it better." With this he left the lab, and I practically did not see him for three months.

I was not alone in the lab with this mountain of machine parts covered by oily blueprints. I was embraced by small, very curious, friendly and extremely helpful crowd—the system engineer, electronic technician, two toolmakers, and the lab supervisor. They had their work to do, but they gladly took me under their wings to show me around. They helped with necessary tools, brought me lots of coffee in paper cups with instant poker pictures on them—the winning card was on the bottom of the cup, so one had to finish the coffee first. They asked me lots of non-technical questions and immersed me in a wonderfully aristocratic New England dialect.

• • •

My grandson Joe was born January 9, 1978, and I became a happy grandfather. A circumcision ritual and procedure were performed in our apartment. Bob looked pretty oozy. A couple of friends carefully held him close to the operation table, and he fainted at the peak moment of sacrifice of his son's flesh.

Bob got his first job at the local electric cable plant. The plant gladly hired newcomers ready to accept the entry-level positions with the pay close to minimum wage. The only way to earn more money was overtime, weekends and holiday work. The first New Year's Eve in this country Bob was working. He showed up shortly before 12 o'clock, raised the glass of champagne, and ran back to work. This time coincided with deterioration in his ulcer. He ended up on the operation table. It was difficult time for the kids, and I wished I was more physically and emotionally available for them in those times of my uncertain and stressful probation.

Gradually they got their rhythm and momentum. After the energy crisis, high inflation and souring interest rates—on the watch of affable and well meaning Jimmy Carter—it was Reagan's time of economic revival and housing boom. Bob decided to flex his muscles. He followed a motto, very popular among Russian emigrants at this moment: "Put into this housing boom all the money you have, and even don't have, and make it work." They would buy dilapidated properties, hire help, or fix them by themselves. They would help each other with financing, cosigning, and putting their security on the line. They would aggressively push and redefine borders of "bad" areas and neighborhoods, and they would recuperate slum areas lost to poverty and neglect during recession and period of "welfare society." The strategy worked for many of them and for the neighborhoods in the mean time. As many of them learned later, this attitude worked only in good times. It worked well because unlike experienced Americans, they just pushed forward without looking back. The only prudent ones saw the right time to get out of the game.

So, Bob moved his family to Boston and got involved in the real estate business. At first, everything was going well. They bought and renovated a big house in Brookline for themselves. My second grandson, Myron, was born in May of

1988. When I visited Bob at his new office, he looked like real businessman, respectable and confident. One thing Bob forgot to consider in his busy time was that success in a capitalistic environment, among other things like luck and opportunity, was dependent upon knowledge, experience, discipline, and also the ability to keep a finger on the pulse of economy. This was something Bob simply disregarded. In fact, he was quite arrogant about the role of education and diligent reading. He considered natural talent the only important trait. This character quality was rare in our ethnic culture. The parents constantly reminded their children that in Diaspora, in the environment of no land and no natural resources at their disposal, they had only one opportunity to survive—to educate. On top of that, Bob got too much taste and fun in creative investment and financing, the very mine infested field, the field requiring strong legal expertise and ethical prudence.

The unraveling of Bob's business didn't wait for long. The economic environment started to reverse. Bob was over-stretched, got broke, and lost everything. He left Lora to deal with pieces of broken life and ran away for a business solution to Russia, an emerging "economic heaven." Russia was a very questionable "heaven" for honest business at that time. The boundless natural wealth of this country was exploited by the bands of Mafia, drug dealers, and government sponsored criminals. The Russian environment was simply not safe in a very physical sense of that word.

Bob migrated from Russia to Austria, back to Russia, then to Spain in an effort to find himself. At certain points he couldn't or didn't choose to avoid some ethical compromises. In the mean time, his loyalty and fidelity to his wife slipped away. His sexual escapades became common. He announced to his children that they had a new brother out of wedlock somewhere in Korea. Lora had faithfully followed her husband everywhere, trying to save the family. But she soon realized that this situation was very detrimental to her health and the moral fabric of her children. She made a decision to leave Bob for good. Fortunately, Joe, going through turmoil, and then torn apart Myron, made the right choice. They fully supported their mother in her decision to file for divorce and return to the United States. Lora, on the brink of a nervous break down went to the Rhode Island School of Design, bought a computer, rented an apartment in Providence, and started from scratch as an interior designer. She got a couple of wonderful loving children on her side and eventually found her happiness and love with a good, caring man. The happy end for my family peeked out on the horizon in a "famous Hollywood tradition."

Joe, fluent in Russian, French, German, Spanish and English, graduated from an international high school in Vienna. Four years later he graduated from New York School in Liberal Art. He started to work as an assistant producer in documentary filmmaking and advertising. Then, just recently, at the age of twenty-six, he founded his own small and very dynamic advertising corporation with distinct international flavor. He is now a proud producer and foot soldier of it. He is showing great drive, creativity and dedication, combined with prudence and fiscal discipline.

At the same time, Joe bought a tiny, dilapidated top-floor studio in the East Village of Manhattan. The apartments in this building had floors that closely resembled famous San Francisco streets. The windows were falling out of the brick walls, turning to dust with the first touch. He, who never done it before; whose father never knew which end of the nail was for the hammer and which for the wall, fixed and radically renovated his apartment to a condition quite livable for a bachelor. He leveled and restored hardwood floor, reset windows, added fireproof window and granite countertop in a kitchenette, and renovated the bathroom. He discovered a tiny fireplace, buried in the wall, and finished it. He could see now the New York sky through the huge skylight he installed on a stripped-to-the-beams ceiling. He even found perfectly suitable "antique" steel staircase somewhere in a trash and could now get on the flat roof with the wonderful city skyline in view. Of course he didn't always keep his nest in a pristine order. But recently, when Lora stayed in his apartment for few days while Joe was away on business, she cleaned it up, rid the refrigerator of months old vegetables and sausages, put things in order, and showed how things were to be done.

An attractive and affable young man—the ladies' sweet-heart—Joe showed a mature, loyal, and determined personality in business and friendships. Joe and I have been very open with each other, up to the very personal points in our lives. Joe often asked me, "Am I too harsh with the girlfriend I don't like any more? Am I too mean with my partners, not willing or not capable sometimes to do an adequate job? Do I have too much of my father's genes in me? What do you think, Deda?"

I showed Joe the photos of him, holding his baby brother like a tender loving father. I assured him that he had always been a loving father figure to the little boy, who missed it so much. "No." I said, "You don't have to worry about that. You have plenty of your mother's genes and strong bones in your spine." I have always cherished an opportunity for such exchanges. I had no doubts that Joe put himself strongly on the right path.

Myron has been another object of my pride. In his multi-facet personality, Myron has been the exact opposite of his brother. If Joe is extroverted and slightly cool about scholar achievements, Myron is introverted. He tried every kind of activity at high school to find what he liked the best. He was involved in the school radio station as a newsman and host. He played in drama, and later he wrote and directed his own play. He played the keyboard, sang in school choir, and then got seriously immersed in classic and modern chorale singing. Like his brother, he is multilingual.

Myron has also been a good and very passionate tennis player with excellent reflexes. I had lots of fun watching the two brothers play; they were so involved in the game (Joe mostly kidding, Myron snapping back). I was not bad for my age in this game. I tried to flex my muscles with them. They praised me, shaking their heads in amazement and approval . . . and beat me to a pulp.

Myron skipped his teen blues. He forgot about them, so much he was busy and involved. He was accepted by the George Washington University in Washington, D.C., and in fall of 2006, he will start his study. "What are you going to choose as your major?" I asked him.

"I don't know yet. I liked everything I touched," he replied.

Myron, in my not unbiased opinion, is a tall, extremely attractive young man with the striking dark eyes and curly hair of our biblical ancestors and the character of an angel.

I was most definitely the biggest winner in our emigration adventure. I got my daughter with me, the loving daughter with ever evolving and growing desire for personal connection.

"Well, daughters must love and respect their fathers . . . period, the end of story." But I could never figure out how and when I earned such love and admiration from my grand-children. Joe grew on my lap till 6 or 8, but then we were separated when my kids were wandering around the world for more than 10 years. Later, when we were occasionally sepa-rated again and I was under great deal of stress in my personal life, they would often call me and ask: "Deda, please let us know if you need anything. We are with you. You know we love you so very much."

• • •

Nick came to the lab with the Company's vice president in exactly three months. The machine was running, and I was ready. There were plenty of weak points and limitations in the current machine design. I told them that I wouldn't expect better performance, particularly for extended machine sizes, without major rethinking and modifications. The audit was a success.

The mountain fell off my shoulders. I have bought a brand new, tan colored Buick Skylark, a Walkman radio, and nice, comfortable sneakers. I worked in my cubicle during the day. Lunchtime was my time to walk, listen to music, news, and lively conversations on a radio. I was gaining my English on top of a Berlitz course, which I took to strengthen my grammar, style and punctuation.

The Harp's forest was spectacular, especially during foli-age. I have seen a lot of New England places with wonderful foliage since, but this forest right around the large parking lot was one of the best. A few years later, my cautious baby brother Ned visited me "for a little site survey."

"Who pruned all these trees on the highway?" he wondered with amazement. "They look like in royal parks of England—where, besides, I've never been."

I had a lot to show him. But the first I did for my visitor was an excursion to Home Depot. Being handymen has always been our tradition. For Ned, the Home Depot was a knockout in the first round. As a result, America got one more handyman, and on the side, an excellent designer in the field of heat, ventilation and air conditioning (HVAC) for schools, tall buildings, and other public places. When we visited New York, Ned would look up at particular building from the street and describe the most likely design of its HVAC system.

Ned settled in Rhode Island on the outskirts of Providence with his wife Raisa, daughter Natasha and the elderly in-laws. The in-laws had retired, and the rest of the family got jobs in their Engineering fields. After few tests and trials Ned landed at the Company in his area of expertise, where, as he said: "Money is not so great, travel to work is longer, but the boss is nice, colleagues are cheerful, and nobody will push me to retire, unless I want to."

People think we are very similar. Maybe he is—I am not. Yes, we maintain the same goatees, but I copied it from my grandfather ... Ned did it from me; I am balding, he is not, and most likely never will. He is extroverted like our father; I'm introverted just like our mother. I am immersed into American culture ... he, although a steadfast American patriot, still likes sometimes to watch Russian movies and listen to Russian news. We both have beautiful daughters and wonderful grandchildren, but in Ned's family, children are "iconized" and idolized; I, however, prefer slightly "cooler" approach.

Our family is marked by a chain of almost bizarre coincidences. My brother and I were born in June, six years and three days apart, under the same sign of Zodiac. As if this accuracy was not enough, my father decided to part this world just between our birthdays. This was ultimate manifestation of his eternal love. So, we celebrate our birthdays and light the candle for our father the same day. We both are "experts" in shish-kebob and Middle Asian pilaf, and play host in turn. But he doesn't know how to make thick foam for cappuccino … I do. On the other hand, Ned is an excellent driver, with his Camry connected directly to his brain, just like his arms and legs. Different or similar, he is still my baby brother and we always there for each other.

chapter 9

I have to apologize, but as a technocrat, I have no choice but to get slightly technical sometimes. I promise though to be as pithy as possible. So, please relax . . .

Any precision machine—be it the car engine, machine tool or aircraft—in order to be assembled and to perform its functions accurately and reliably, has to be made of parts perfectly matching each other. The better the dimensional accuracy of these parts, the better, longer, and more reliable the machine performance.

In order to accurately manufacture these parts, we have to measure them periodically to make sure that manufacturing process doesn't break down and produce faulty parts. The measuring machine comes to the aid as the most sophisticated tool. It measures these parts by touching different points of them with the probe and sending the information about these points' exact location to the computer. The computer then processes this information and "tells" us how accurate the part is.

To measure accurately enough, however, the probe must

be, *first*, free of vibrations, which can come from drives, shop floor, or from machine inertial forces. Only when this *dynamic accuracy* is achieved, we can talk about the *second* requirements for accurate measurements, i.e. the precise knowledge about probe location, or *the geometric accuracy*. This problem can be solved by means of precision laser or optical measuring systems.

The probe can be moved around the part manually. In the computer-controlled machines, however, it moves, touches the part, and takes measurements automatically.

My first project at Harp Manufacturing was to improve dynamic and geometric accuracy of the tabletop measuring machine, the one I had for my "probation," to expand its size and convert it from manual mode to a direct computer control. I redesigned and put the machine into production. It was on the market for broad variety of sizes for about 6 years. The basic machine's mechanical core was sounder and more reliable, with some cost problems to be resolved later. The cost issues, or more precisely, the balance between the machine's functional quality and cost, became a most challenging aspect of my work.

With my first success came recognition from the company's management and—most precious—from my colleagues. In their eyes I wasn't a fuzzy Siberian bear anymore, descending from my tree to teach Americans how to design. The president of the company, Dan Raush, was frequent visitor to the lab and to the assembly floor, asking me to explain to his guests how this machine worked. The facial profile of an intense looking man, aiding his lectures with heavy ethnic gesticulations, appeared in the technical news and marketing papers.

My first encounter with Dan was way back at the company's Christmas party of 1977, right after I was hired. Dan was walking around the tables with employees and guests, greeting everyone with small talk. I didn't know yet who he was. My turn came, and Dan asked me the question I heard many times:

"How do you like America?"

"That's a silly question," I replied in my "perfect" English.

Dan slapped my shoulder and laughed aloud. The whole table laughed with him.

"What's wrong?" I asked my friends.

"Did you know who it was?"

"I have no idea."

"It was our president, Dan Raush, you were talking "silly"" to."

It was my Russian background talking, though. My friends had no idea that the workplace environment in Russia was probably the most "democratic" one. In order to be fired in the Soviet society of ideological *full employment*, one had to be something much more than just "silly," incompetent, drunk, or lazy. The intent to emigrate, however, would often qualify for dismissal and a firm place in the black book of no redemption. In the mean time, everyone in Russia could send his boss to hell, or even further, with no recourse—the boss had often not much to do with promotion, demotion or dismissal. There were the other more important hiring factors to consider, like, for example, a faithful service in the Communist Party. This "democratic" instinct haunted me for some time in my new and indeed most democratic country, though with a different and much more complicated working relationship structure.

With success came also the most gratifying realization: now it was not just I who gained benefits of this country; now the country was also getting something from me. I was determined to make my give-and-take balance as positive as possible. At some point I became restless. Fixing old machines was not what I dreamed of. I visualized *my* machine, the sleek, classic, charcoal-gray beauty; the focus point of sophisticated metrology labs at Ford, Mercedes and Boeing; the machine running on its frictionless air bearings with flying speed and taking a hundred measurements per minute.

In the high-speed machine, though, the dynamic performance becomes problem number one. Would I have an opportunity to study the intricate details of dynamic behavior of the structure, which is changing every time when a measuring probe moves along the part in its work space? It's like dealing with infinite number of machines within a single structure. And on the top of it, no single machine can be sold if it is not accurate, not reliable and expensive. In other words, as marketing put it: "It should look like a stick with couple rubber bands, and work at cosmic speed like a charm."

But those dreams had to be put on the backburner for quite awhile. In October of 1982, the Labor Union initiated a bitter strike against Harp Manufacturing after the company refused to bargain in "good faith." Harp's employees suddenly found themselves in the middle of the battle zone. Picketers burned trash in big steel barrels at the company's entrance, day and night; attacked the cars of non-union members (management, clerical, engineering, etc.,) with rocks; and threatened physical harm to them and even to their families if they crossed the line. One day some members of the Teamster Union showed up in solidarity, playing with their mighty biceps and shouting obscenities. Police sprayed pepper gas on some 800 picketers. Three weeks later, a machinist narrowly escaped serious injury when a shot fired into the picket line hit his belt buckle.

The strike came out to be formally the longest in national history, but eventually it subsided. Many strikers were replaced and found other jobs. The company's workforce was streamlined, and even the company's structure changed. During the peak of the strike, everyone capable to move worked on the assembly line, putting together parts made outside the company.

I couldn't judge about fairness of negotiations—nobody invited me to the table—but I witnessed how harmful the union attitude was to the company's competitive survival. The union was shooting itself in the foot. Their members flatly refused to do anything that wasn't their direct contractual responsibility. At the end of the months or quarters, when maximum effort should have been put into assembly, crating and shipment—and the machinists, by the way, didn't have anything to do—they refused to give a hand. They would just stand and watch. As a result, the company often failed to deliver and was losing money.

During the energy crisis and the peak of the strike, Harp's management employees were forced to carpool. One of the members of our carpool teams was Bruce McKinney, my neighbor, colleague, and the first American friend of my family. Skinny, athletic, hyperactive, and at the same time, incredibly sensitive and intuitive, Bruce was living the fast life. He was an electronic engineer by trade, and his driving was appropriately of "sinusoidal" pattern, and at 20 - 30 above the speed limit. He graciously maneuvered between cars at that speed, never cutting off and never caught by the police. I kept my eyes closed and fists tight when Bruce was behind the wheel. But Bruce wasn't one, who was dangerous on the road.

He admitted later, rather reluctantly, that my slow but not always predictable driving made him very nervous. I may have had my good angel always with me—for 28 years of driving in America, I had only one minor accident, when I showed my blinking lights too late. "Please, don't leave me, angel, at least not yet!"

Bruce couldn't tolerate slow life. He moved to marketing and then formed his company, providing software service for the measuring machine users. He ended his life tragically. Bruce's partner, the software developer, got disenchanted with their business arrangement. When Bruce offered him a fair way out—Bruce never mixed friendship with business—his partner shot him on their business trip to Mexico. The killer tried to simulate kidnapping for ransom by Mexicans, but police found matching shells in his rural house yard in Rhode Island, which he used as a shooting range. He has been serving his life sentence in a Mexican jail, not the best place to enjoy your time. Bruce's image has been visiting me pretty often.

. . .

Finally, the "Day of Judgment" came. Nick Cook ordered his designers to come out with proposals for new super-machine, the company's next moneymaker. My proposal won. My main Marketing challenge was now to keep costs down and to not compromise on machine accuracy, measuring speed, reliability and appearance. The biggest technical problem was to make it dynamically stable for any machine size, even one the size of the house. This modest word "stable," often lost among others in marketing documents, in fact represented the very essence of a new machine called "MCell."

In order to make overextended machine dynamically stable, it should have been structurally analyzed for every size, and individually tuned with special damping and energy absorbing devices. Progress in the development of computer-aided tools in structural dynamic analysis came to my aid. It was as challenging as an automobile gas turbine engine I created for the diploma project of my youth. I encapsulated myself in my office with the computers and special software.

In the mean time, the company's best toolmaker, Jeff Langly, was assigned to my project. Jeff became my faithful and indispensable helper and friend. Like famous "Lefty" from Russian folk tales, capable of putting a shoe on a foot of the flea, Jeff was left-handed, and he could do exactly that.

Nick Cook got very actively involved in the details of the project. His technical suggestions were very useful. His help in communication with different suppliers of materials and technological processes was indispensable. I wasn't very comfortable in this kind of logistical activity yet, and Nick sensed that. Later he liked to crack proud jokes about my hiring as "his greatest accomplishment." But I never failed to appreciate Nick's direct contribution in my work, and most of all, his open mind and the role he played in my professional future. I realized that if I had bumped at Harp into another "Mr.Partosh" of my very first and failed interview, my professional career could have turned out very different and much less productive.

The first prototype of a new machine was being built in the Lab. I kept one eye on what Jeff was doing in assembly and in processes of the extruded aluminum rails and air bearings manufacturing with different surface treatments. But my major concern was my new self-tuning seismic energy absorbing system as a tool of dynamic stability.

In the mean time, the company hired a young, seemingly talented and slightly snobbish engineer, Mark Lando, from Livermore National Lab. His project was to further extend my previous machine by improving tunable hydraulic damper, which I designed for this machine at the beginning of my tenure. I didn't expect much of an output from his effort—damper, in my opinion, was reaching its limits—but it may have been some backup for me, if my absorber failed and his damper succeeded.

Common wisdom says that bad news always come in bunches. When my prototype was about ready and I still struggled with some problems with my absorber, the following events happened all at the same time: Nick Cook left engineering for marketing; John Jackson, the former designer of original machine (remember the skid with the mountain of parts?) took his place; Mark failed with his honest effort, didn't want to deal with somebody else's "crap" any more (I don't blame him, even if this "crap" is mine), and quit. Frustrated, John came out with *simple* decision: "If you don't make your machine work in two weeks, Jay, I will dump the project."

Just when I was watching a ceiling cave in on me, Dan Raush, the president, came to the rescue. Two days after my encounter with John I received a phone call from Dan: "Show me your machine … now." He listened to me, looked at the machine, at this beast I was so much in love with, and said: "Don't worry, Jay, just make it work. I like it. I think it's going to fly."

The early morning was the time when the best ideas, if any, would normally come to my mind. The next day after Dan visited the lab, my usual friend, the Good Angel, woke me up with the best idea I've ever had. It was a seismic inertial energy absorber solution so simple that it solved dynamic problems for a machine of any specified size. It was patented soon separately and as the part of my machine, and it made MCell "fly high."

My relationship with managing personnel was always mixed. My Russian "democratic work place" background often bulged out. At first I was an amusing guest at some private management gatherings. Later, when my English improved and I could express what I thought, the invitations wound down. So did my prospects to climb the management ladder. But I was happy in my tiny cell and enjoyed my creative work. In a heavy air of management politics, I would be like a fish out of water.

I had very good friends among my colleagues and helpers. My relationship with workers on the assembly line was particularly warm. With one of my colleagues, Ghon Tai, I developed a particularly close working alliance. Ghon came to America from China on a student exchange program and made his Ph.D. thesis in optics. He was working on an optical probing project. But he was also very good in practical computer application for development and production, and he got involved in the application of my MCell Floor Vibration Response study. We lived in the same neighborhood and developed a close personal friendship. We played volleyball, tennis and billiards together and exchanged Russian and Chinese vodkas. I called his little round-faced and bold-headed son Rubi "the Chinese Emperor"; and Ghon showed me how to find a Chinese restaurant with fresh and natural food. Later, when I was leaving the company, Ghon made big plaque out of the machine Logo plate, attached a fancy silhouette of a designer sitting at the old fashion drawing board with a word "Unforgettable" above it, and collected hundreds of signatures spread all over the plaque.

"What did you mean by 'Unforgettable'?" I wondered.

"You know better; you are an expert in vibes," he replied with an enigmatic smile and encouraging applause at the banquet table. Shortly after, Ghon himself left Harp and got involved in fiber optics.

Sales and marketing treated me like a celebrity, especially after the successful show. The salesmen admired good wine and lobsters, celebrating fat sales. Sometimes during the shows they would invite me for the dinners. They would teach me how to choose good wine, how to sniff a cork for the wine test, and how to select a proper appetizer or main dish. The food and wine were very good, and nothing could be more pleasant than a company of happy salesmen looking into your mouth, but I didn't remember any of these "gourmet" lessons. My favorite has always been a fresh New York bagel with cream cheese, lox, and glass of white Zinfandel—nice and simple.

The heartwarming recognition came also from the academic world. One day I attended a conference of the Society of Mechanical Engineering. The agenda covered a broad spectrum of lectures and workshops from a dynamic stability of super long and "flimsy" space manipulators used to build a space lab ... to a baby field of Nano-technology—the field of genetically self-reproducing machines at molecular size. I was wandering between different rooms, trying to find the most enticing event. One lecture was about machine tool and measuring machine metrology. The lecturer was Professor Rupert Bocken, the gregarious professor of one of the leading universities and the former head of the department of metrology at the Institute of Standards. During his time at the Institute, his department was involved in vigorous tests of one of MCell's prototypes.

I carefully entered the room in the middle of the lecture and lowered myself into the nearest chair in the back row.

"I normally don't encourage my students to enter in the middle of the lectures. I make some exceptions, though," said the professor, facing the blackboard and looking into my corner with a Cyclopus's eye located somewhere on the back of his head. Then he turned to the audience ... and introduced me with a couple of nice words.

My machine was a major company product for almost fifteen years. This was unusual for our dynamic high-tech environment. I was involved now in some improvements, extensions and special applications, using my well developed by that time structural analysis apparatus. I also conducted some tests of vibration isolation systems, offered by different vendors in application of my machine to harsh machine shop floors. My knowledge in machine dynamic response was instrumental in these tests. Life became more "academic" and relaxed. Nobody bothered me. My occasional inputs here and there were enough to keep me on modest payroll. I could probably work quietly for few years left for retirement, and perhaps even beyond. Not for the infamous Jay Khmelinsky, though.

I was thinking about a new, much faster and more accurate machine. Nobody asked me about that. Marketing was happy. "Why bother?" was their thinking. I talked about this idea to my "Lefty" friend, nevertheless. Jeff got so enthusiastic that he made the table size model of this machine out of aluminum in his free time. I asked for a special meeting to present my ideas and show this model—to no avail. The 20-pound model became my home souvenir, following me in my retirement wherever I moved.

"Is this the machine you designed? It's a beauty!" my grandson Joe once asked me.

"Well, not exactly. This was one I haven't," I replied.

The economic environment for American manufacturing turned sour. Harp's former subsidiaries in Italy and Germany became major suppliers of measuring machines, quite naturally offering their own solutions. The Harp Manufacturing slowly slipped into a position of mostly marketing and sales. I didn't wait until my "talent" in sales would be called for, or somebody would offer me, *God forbid*, some severance for graceful retirement. I just quit at the age of sixty-two.

I idled not for too long, though. One of the struggling vendors of Vibration Isolation Systems, Gene Hammer, a savvy salesman and engineer, my old friend and wonderful man of integrity and hard work, offered me to design a new system based on my experience with theirs and other systems' tests at Harp. A small group of four enthusiasts formed a tiny corporation with a designer, salesman, serviceman, and an executive officer. I have designed, tested, modified, tested again and patented new systems. I found a small and very dynamic shop run by the band of dedicated Vietnamese brothers, willing to fairly reasonably manufacture it when it was needed—far not every machine required vibration isolation, only ones which had to be placed right in the midst of the floor with a heavy production machinery. And when a call would come, we were ready. A good number of mine and other machines sold by Harp and other companies were equipped by the new vibration isolation system. And I couldn't recall any complaints from the customers ... yet.

I settled with my second wife, Mary, in Western Arizona, in the Tri-state area, just where the states of California, Nevada and Arizona happily meet in a bustling casino and golfing center. I was neither gambling nor playing Golf, but rather enjoying year-round sun, stars and scenery, playing tennis and walking my dog. My office was always nearby on my laptop, and when my help was needed, I was always there.

I would visit Harp every time I was back to New England on business or to see my kids. I missed some of my buddies. Marketing was still there. One of my teachers in cork-sniffing technique gave me a *bear-hug* last time and said:

"When we heard about Russian Bear, coming years ago to help us to compete, we wondered—from which tree outside our windows would he jump right into our office?"

"And how did it look when he landed on your desk?"

"With this goatee of yours? He looked like a darn Ph.D. from MIT."

Nick Cook has been coming often to my mind. I called him once in awhile, always with some degree of trepidation:

"Are you still measuring miles of this world, my old friend? So glad to hear your voice, Nick."

"I couldn't find my grave site yet, Jay. It must be somewhere in the crowd of my relatives from Scotland, settled here in the eighteenth century. Why don't you stop by next time, young man? We would get together with a bunch of our old guards and have a couple beers and laughs. I will show you my new acquisition—the Civil War rifle. It's a beauty."

chapter 10

I met her in early spring of 1981 at an amateur performance of "Camelot," performed in one of the Rhode Island churches. It was the cultural festival, attended by the University Society of Rhode Island, the group of single professionals I had recently joined. She was sitting across the big round table, occasionally talking to the man on her right. She struck me with rear sense of dignity and beauty: face outline, blue eyes and silver hair, little touch of make-up, classic neatly selected dress, mild aristocratic manners and quiet smile. I couldn't take my eyes off her for the whole evening. She noticed that. Her eyes would stop on me slightly longer, and a hardly noticeable smile would touch her lips.

"What a lucky man!" I thought about her escort.

After the show, we gathered for a cocktail party at the house of one of the members of our group. She was there and mostly alone, standing with a cigarette at the open door to the balcony—her escort was busy with somebody else. I asked for a dance, and we talked. I noticed that in dance, Mary—this was her name—wouldn't let me lead, but rather resisted and initiated her own path. I had difficulty adapting and stepped on her toes a few times.

"Sorry, I'm dancing like clumsy Siberian bear."

"That's all right," she replied with her soft and sexy low-tone voice and smiled.

"Your escort abandoned you, Mary," I mentioned carefully.

"He just gave me a ride. I don't drive on the highway," she replied.

It took a full week before I dared to call her. I was very nervous. But she, in her very genteel way, made me feel at ease. I invited her for coffee and a walk in the park. I took a beautiful picture of her sitting on the bench, half turned toward me, with her usual cigarette and coquettish smile. We met each other often, went to the festivals, plays, concerts and parks, or just sat close to each other on a porch of her apartment in North Providence and talked. This dark porch was the place where after a couple months of courting, we made love for the first time.

She was divorced and lived in her apartment with her two boys, 10-year-old Elmer and 17-year-old Bernie. She told me that her former husband couldn't make anything out of their life. They were constantly in suitcases, moving from place to place, and she left him after she learned about his infidelity.

"Did you ever love him?" I asked. "Had he ever made you happy as a person, as a lover?"

"Not really. He was a miserable failure."

"Why did you marry him?"

"It was time, and I had my miseries too"

"From one misery to another," I summarized.

"Just about," she responded.

She seemed to be uncomfortable talking about her marriage failure. At the moment of break-up, as I learned much later, she dropped out of sight. With two little children having some health problems, and with some serious medical issues of her own, she made an almost fatal decision. Instead of staying close to her extended family, she secluded herself with children in somebody's abandoned trailer, living with no decent food and without running water and electricity. Nobody could find her for long time—she left no address to anyone. Somehow her sisters found her sick and delirious and pulled her out to Rhode Island, where one of her sisters lived at that time. It took a long time and two serious operations for Mary to recuperate and get on her feet.

This was my first very confusing lesson of Mary's denial, submission to stigma, and deliberate isolation. I took it at first more as a manifestation of pride and dignity. Only later I realized how difficult to the family relationship this attitude could be.

She was originally from the old little town of Newcastle in Delaware. Her mix was British and French. Some of her Quaker ancestors landed in this country not much after the legendary Mayflower. Her family was originated from one of the clan members, expelled from the Quaker ranks for some minor violations of the strict rules of their society. As a result, her family never rose to any prominence and lived with very modest means. Later, when we were already married, Mary and her two older sisters were discovered as the only living relatives of their prominent great grandaunt, the founder of many charitable foundations, universities and hospitals in Pennsylvania. The sisters were the dignitaries at a big anniversary gala, and Mary talked about it with pride. She even got involved in genealogy research of her family but didn't get far—the enthusiasm faded somewhere in the middle of the process.

Bit by bit, I also learned that her father was a bitter failure, an alcoholic and an abuser. He aspired to be a banker, but for some reason he ended up doing a menial job at the factory. Weekends after the bar were the times of his rage. His first target was their mother, basically, as Mary said, a very nice and cheerful woman. He brutalized her in front of the girls until she had a mental break down and multiple heart attacks. She died at the age of 40. After the wife's death, the father turned his rage on the girls. The oldest one was now target number one. Father watched her every step, beat her up, called her derogatory names, and didn't rest until she ended up in a mental institution. She was repeatedly raped there, gave birth to a couple of boys—grown up, nevertheless, to become fine men and successful entrepreneurs—and didn't live long. Two of Mary's sisters were lucky, though. They managed to get strong protectors. The boyfriends put big fists under the father's nose, married the girls, and pulled them out of the house. They were decent, hardworking, beer drinking blue-collar guys, and they maintained their strong traditional families.

Mary was now alone, facing her father at the age of fifteen. They had lots of relatives in the immediate neighborhood, but nobody ever knew or wanted to know what was going on in Mary's family. Only much later, when all this abuse already had taken a heavy toll on her health, Mary opened to me a little door into her life at that stage. Her escape from the misery was the little town library, where she read every single book. Later it was a School of Radiological Technology, where she stayed at dormitory, earned a little stipend, babysat, and lived on crackers, canned soups, cigarettes and coffee.

I had an occasion to visit Mary's townhouse in Newcastle at some point. The place looked not much better than my apartment in Moscow, which we had after WWII. The outhouse in Newcastle, though, was somewhat more sophisticated and wasn't a communal one like in Moscow. The realization that Mary, just like I, knew real hardship in her life, drew me closer to her. The effect of these hardships on our characters, as I learned later, was different, though. Mary always surrounded herself with "things": furniture, books, clothes and shoes. I, however, could live with very minimal sufficient comfort and always rejected anything superfluous.

So apparently we were from families with similarly meager means of living. But what a striking contrast between two fathers: one who created an environment of love and security, another - the atmosphere of hate and horror! I had no idea at that point what would be an effect of Mary's upbringing on her character, on her emotional state, and even her very ability to love anybody but a toddler or little dog. I had a lot to learn in years to come.

In the mean time, it didn't take long before I found myself deeply in love. I had introduced Mary to my friends. They were impressed with her remarkable lady-like beauty and quiet grace. Some of them took this union as a revolution and an example to follow. Mary was intrigued and very pleasant but slightly aloof.

We dated for about a year, and I was driving frequently back and forth. Sometimes I was coming home very late and quite tired. One day I fell asleep right on the bridge over the railroad and woke up on the opposite side of the road. Shortly after, I bought a sapphire engagement ring—Mary liked sapphires. I told Mary: "You marry me right now, or I will get killed."

She said: "I love you, too," and often reminded me that I never knelt on my knee and performed a formal proposal.

The wedding was at a cozy lounge of an Italian restaurant in East Greenwich. I was a frequent guest at this restaurant, and I knew its owner. The restaurant seldom had such an event in its lounge, and it made the wedding very pleasant and homey. The restaurant owner and his son played piano "four-hand" for this special occasion. Everything was spontaneous, without a rehearsal and, of course, not without some minor procedural problems. My friend Bruce was my best man. In the middle of a ceremony, bewildered four-year-old Joe couldn't stand something "terrible" happening to his Deda. He ran to the stage, grabbed my leg, and didn't let it go until the end of the ceremony. I picked him up, and we all three got married together.

I moved the whole family into my house, but Bernie soon left for Rochester Institute of Technology to study Computer Science, the thing he fooled around with since he was little. Elmer, though, had to adapt to his new father.

My relationship with Elmer wasn't easy at the beginning. Elmer was introverted with a very strong passive resistance to any intrusion into his inner self. He didn't talk back but would never do what he didn't like. He struggled with some learning disabilities, lagged in science, and his hand had a tremor when he was writing. This was making his writing almost illegible. But when he had to draw a line in the art class, it was very confident and precise. We never had a chance to get to the root of his problems.

Disability, as I could sense, made Elmer angry. The happy grin of his elementary school faded from his face. Growing up without biological father didn't help, either. Normally Elmer kept his emotions to himself. But sometimes, the object of his anger was Joe, who visited and even stayed in our house quite often. Was it partly a competition for love and attention? I didn't know at that point. Elmer hit Joe once pretty hard when he was thirteen and eight years older than Joe—different league. I admit I was oblivious to their conflict, or played it down, and learned more about it much later from Joe. I remember how I tossed my five-year-old brother Ned under the table when he was asking for too much attention at a busy moment. Maybe this had disqualified me as a fair judge.

The truth is known: "If you need true friend, get a dog." And Elmer had one. We had a gorgeous black Great Dane. I bought her from the private owner as a puppy before my marriage. Bonny was an un-trainable disaster in the house. The objects of her retaliation, when she was alone, were rugs, carpets, tablecloths, pillows, wallpaper, etc. She listened only to Elmer when they were alone together. She pulled him on the bike by the leash all over our community. She died suddenly from intestinal blockage, common for these big dogs. Poor creature apparently suffered from so much pain that she made our house on both floors look like a tornado had hit. Elmer suffered greatly but showed remarkable stoicism.

Later I learned another trait in Elmer's abilities. Elmer was around fourteen when I brought home from work some complex drawings to study. Elmer happened to stand behind me, looking over my shoulder. As soon as I opened the blue print, Elmer asked me a bunch of questions—he figured out in a quick moment how this mechanism worked.

Elmer didn't complete his regular high school. Academic study wasn't his motto. The teachers recommended vocational school instead, where Elmer learned machining, tool making, and machine assembly. Later, when Elmer lived in his own house in the countryside, he would surround himself with junk cars, driving his neighbors crazy. He never read manuals, but he would always be able to put together for himself or for his friends a well functioning vehicle, made out of parts from different cars. He worked first at General Dynamics' Submarine Assembly plant. And then for a good number of years he has been working as a valuable toolmaker and assembler of recycling machines for a small dynamic company in Rhode Island.

As a child, and then as adult, Elmer was always stuck around losers and the needy. He did it apparently not from weakness or low self-esteem but from a natural desire to help. Neighboring kids from dysfunctional families would lean on him and like his "cool" demeanor. As an adult he had a few relationships with worthless, welfare-addicted single mothers. He was always a steady and patient guardian to those children. But this charity never aided any stability in his own life. Finally he met a serious and hard working divorcee with two well-fostered boys. They joined their households and formed a happy family. They bought two canoes—their house was close to a big lake—some fishing gear and camping equipment to enjoy the simple life.

It would normally take some effort for me to pool a single word out of Elmer. But if help was needed, he was the guy. In one of his Father's Day cards to me Elmer wrote: "You were like a father to me." To get this from Elmer meant something.

Bernie was directly opposite of his brother. An ordinary whiz, soft spoken, intelligent computer guru, he has been working for a major computer game developing company in Canada. He and his Russian girl friend—some examples are addictive—have a little girl, Sarah, who is Mary's joy. Mary kept a collection of her pictures and videos, comparable in volume only to the American National Archives. Bernie had some turbulent periods in his life at college time and right after. He sought counseling, got serious, and kept things under control. He has been working on complex projects, functioning normally, and is emotionally stable and happy.

• • •

Our honeymoon was a round car trip in a car: Acadia National Park, Nova Scotia (on a ferry), Cape Breton, Prince Edward Island, and the Bay of Fundy. There is no need to describe the spectacular coastal ride of Breton, the pastoral fields of Edward, and the stone formations of Fundy with miles of tide. One has to see it for himself. Mary enjoyed the trip. She liked the scenery and particularly the quaint little inns and bed-and-breakfasts on Breton. She seemed to be very happy and affectionate. But I noticed that when it came to intimacy, she was tight and apologetic. Only almost at the tour end, at the camp of Fundy, I held in my arms a woman from my fantasies.

Shortly upon our return home from the trip Mary started to complain about excessive fatigue and bodily pain. Going from North Kingstown to a hospital in Providence, where she was working as radiological technologist, was more difficult than from nearby North Providence. It was a long ride, with the bus change in Providence—she still didn't drive car on the highway. It was also more difficult for her to push portable x-ray unit. Finally she took a pay cut, requesting a transfer to the stationary unit. This didn't work, either. One day Mary hurt her back, trying to turn the patient in some emergency situation. Frustrated, she didn't bother to fight for worker's compensation and just quit.

She got involved in crafts, experimented with marbling techniques, and made lots and lots of items she designed and produced for consignment sale. People liked it and praised her for good taste and imagination, but nobody was buying. Some of these artifacts she just gave away as gifts to somebody she knew or used to decorate our house. Mary also tried some fabric application and quilting. She filled up drawers with different tools and fabric odds and ends, and then she lost interest. Mary had some artistic talent, very good sense of color and initial enthusiasm, but probably not enough follow up persistence and business skill to succeed in this tough field. The products of her short-lived enthusiasm have accumulated and never seen the trash can, in hope for a "better day."

It was apparent that something was going on with Mary's health. Visits to multiple doctors didn't do much. Diagnoses varied between depression and Fibromyalgia, or both. The first word Mary didn't want to hear. The second hadn't even been recognized at that time in medical literature as an illness.

Years back at the stage of search for my bachelor house I used to drive sometimes by the "impossible dream" area, which I couldn't even touch at that time. It was the Johnson Pond region with the watershed and tall clear pine trees, reminding me of the pristine area of a summer log cabin in Moscow suburb—the house my family built before WWII and never had a chance to use. In 1986, with some benefits of my stable job, good bonus for my machine, and the right economic situation, I came back to this dream, now for the whole family. Our real estate agent worked hard for us. One day she called me: "There is a house in Wood Estates on Johnson Pond. The situation is unusual, even tragic—the owner has to move in a hurry. The house is not on the market yet, but it will go in a minute. You don't want to miss it."

It was a split-level, three-bedroom contemporary house with a walk-in family room on a slope, overlooking a quiet cove. With the only access under the low clearance bridge, this cove had beautiful vegetation, attracting ducks, geese, herons, and even swans. I could always get on the open main lake with my canoe or Jon boat, but no water skier could get under the bridge, make noise, and cut my water lilies. In still moon nights, I loved to get my canoe out to the middle of the lake and sit there, or lie on the bottom of the boat, watch the sky, and listen to the nightlife.

In the winter, water was partially drained for maintenance purposes, and our cove would become a safe skating rink.

Even wild mushrooms, for some mysterious reason, tended to crowd in a natural part of my yard and around the stumps, as if they knew that this Russian was the only guy around who could tell good mushrooms from bad.

There was a huge oak tree in the middle of our yard. During a Hurricane Gloria, Mary and I witnessed a mini tornado passing our yard toward the cove. It didn't touch our house, brushed this tree, twisted its crown, and broke it in half right in front of our eyes. This tornado, as we learned after the hurricane, passed trough one street with tall trees, knocked down lots of them, and damaged plenty of houses. A couple of houses were literally cut in half by these trees. My next-door neighbor had his part of the scare. The huge pine tree fell right along his house and just brushed the wall by its branches. One of the thick, lonely brunches was buried so deep that we were not able to get it out.

I learned how good the neighborhood cooperation was in a time of natural disaster like this. A few neighbors with chainsaws and other tools showed up in my yard from out of nowhere. They helped to sort out this tree in a few hours. I didn't even know the names of some of my helpers. This tree supplied our two fireplaces with wood for a good few years of regular use. This was one of many cultural shocks I experienced with a great deal of pleasant aftertaste. The next day I helped my neighbor with the tree that graciously missed his house. This neighbor—George was his name—came first to my aid the day before, without even thinking about his problem. He broke his chainsaw on my monstrous oak tree.

I left the stump of this tree intact, put a large flower pot on it, and watered it regularly without any special thoughts about what is going on at the bottom. In the second year after the hurricane, the lush cover of "Opyatas"—the wild mushrooms known as some of the best for frying with potatoes—popped up around this stump. My harvest, just from this stump, was up to three full buckets of mushrooms every year. I brought some fried mushrooms to my neighbors as an example of Russian "organic cuisine."

"See, I ate them, and I am still alive," I tried to convince. They thanked me politely but probably never touched them.

Everything about our house, except something strictly controlled by nature, seemed to be perfect. Well, not so fast— life always had its own rules and plans. And it played out this time, as usual, due to its own agenda.

The pond level was managed by the dam, which belonged to an old mill. One day, the zealous tax hawks from the town of Coventry decided to significantly raise tax on this mill. The mill owners considered it unreasonable and refused to accept. The town insisted. Then the mill drained the Johnson Pond in the middle of the summer, and not just for a short time—for more than a year. This act of an innocent tax dispute worked like ecological sabotage. The flora of the lake has completely changed. When water came back, the gorgeous lilies practically disappeared, overcome and overgrown by weeds.

On top of it, the water sport revolution came to the world. Everyone was riding wave-runners. The low clearance bridge wasn't any obstacle for them. Runners would come in gangs, cut all the weeds, and disappear with triumphant shrieks. The debris would all eventually come to my shores—wind was always toward me—and decay with a horrendous stench. My regular morning exercise from that point on was to rake these weeds with a clam digger. I even bought an expensive mud pump... this didn't work either. I felt like Syziphus, the infamous character of Greek mythology, who was condemned for his sins to roll big bolder on a top of the mountain, let it go down, and roll it up again and again. In 1993 I had had it. We sold our "swamp house" and bought another one in the same area, not on the water, though. We still had our tall pine trees but missed the waterfront with ducks and herons.

On the personal front, things also took an unhappy turn. In the last years in our house on the pond, Mary was growing more and more detached and secluded. She would sit in the upper-floor bedroom most of the day alone, reading and watching the lake activity. In our new house, away from the pond, nothing changed, except she missed her ducks.

During the first ten years of our marriage, we traveled quite a bit around the world. We made Caribbean and Alaskan ship cruses and a bus cruise around the states of Arizona, Utah, Wyoming, Colorado, and New Mexico, including some major national parks along the way. We traveled to England, France, Holland, Belgium, Germany, and Austria. I took Mary with me to Zurich, Switzerland, where my measuring machine was one of the hits at the International Metrology

Show. After the show, we spent a couple of weeks traveling in Switzerland.

With the deterioration in Mary's health and emotional condition, this activity wound down. I tried to make our home as pleasant and comfortable as possible to compensate for the loss of outside activity and stimulation. Our yard was well tended. At home I was always available to help, to cater, to cook, to clean, and to provide transportation to doctor's appointments and other places. Mary was very tense in the car—a classic backseat driver. This oppressive cloud of tension didn't help me enjoy even short car travel with Mary. She explained her tension by the post trauma effect of the accident she had in her youth, when she was thrown out of the car through the windshield. True or something more, I didn't know, but this made us more and more isolated in the house.

We had a basketball hoop, diving pool, spa, and billiards in our new house. I hoped my kids would visit us and enjoy it, but they sensed something was wrong. They didn't want to be a source of tension and were reluctant to visit.

Mary didn't maintain any friendships. "If I go to somebody, then I have to be a host, too. I am not always ready for that, or for any other activity on a short notice for this matter. You know how difficult it is for me," she explained. So in my connection to the outside world I was becoming more like an eligible single, and my friends stopped asking how Mary was doing. Thoughts about infidelity never crossed my mind, although moments of intimacy were becoming more a thing of the past. My suggestions about some counseling were met with the usual denial. Even family counseling for both of us she rejected. Her answer was: "You need it to cope with my illness; I don't"

Every doctor who mentioned the word "depression" was

immediately dumped. She could tolerate nothing but seclusion. Mary's background of abuse, in my own opinion, fired back as a Post Traumatic Stress Syndrome. Her refusal to recognize and address the problem made it more and more difficult for me to handle. My patience and hope were running thin. Everything that would constitute marriage—the emotional, physical, intellectual interaction—was finally grinding to a halt. Could something be done short of separation? Desperate, I decided to try something radical.

• • •

Mary's sisters found a nice area for snow birding. It was in a sunny, dry and winter-warm Colorado River Valley of Western Arizona. The town name was Bullhead City. It had a history that deserved some attention. The town was settled on the Arizonian side of the Colorado River, right at the point where Nevada intruded between the western riverbank and state of California. This formed the "Tri-state" region. The Colorado River, with the mountain ranges on both sides, created beautiful Colorado River Valley.

The initial reason for the town settlement was to support gold and silver mining towns along the range of the Black Mountains of Arizona. In 1953, by the time the mines were exhausted, the Davis Dam was built in the area with an electric power station. It formed the Lake Mohave as a southern part of a gigantic park, Lake Mead National Recreational Area, with the Hoover Dam and Lake Mead above in the north. As a result, the Bullhead City region got an injection of nice recreational potential; and nobody saw it better than young Las Vegas entrepreneur Don Laughlin. One day in 1964, he was flying a little plane over the Bullhead City area and spotted a tiny inn on the Nevada bank of the river. He liked what he saw and bought the inn with a large parcel of the river bank. This was the beginning of Laughlin—one of the major gambling centers of Nevada. Soon, a couple of bridges, new modern roads, Wal-Mart, Home Depot, Office Max, a small international airport (with flights to Mexico as the only "international" destination so far) and lots of other services and businesses followed.

In 1997, when I visited Bullhead City for the first time, the bustling strip of the Las Vegas type casinos reflected in the stream of the Colorado River. The area was recently discovered by the thousands of retirees from all over the country, and particularly by the Baby Boomers from California. Weather, scenery, gambling, and an opportunity for water sports—what else did the California "tired-retired" need to be happy? The housing industry moved in on both sides of the river, building beautiful and relatively inexpensive Mediterranean and Adobe style houses—the ground here never freezes, and houses don't require basements and elaborate foundations. Conditions were ripe, and the whole area took off.

At that point, my isolation system was in production, and my office could travel with me in a briefcase and on the chip of my laptop computer. I thought the warm climate and association with her sisters would perk Mary up, and decided to give it a try.

The sisters spent the wintertime in a little gated retirement community called Siesta Resort. The original history of this particular community was quite extraordinary, almost bizarre. Years ago, a group of Las Vegas entertainers and entrepreneurs got an idea to persuade Arizona to accept gambling in a broad Nevada sense. They were so confident that they bought a big parcel of land in Bullhead City, about 8–10 miles down the river from the Laughlin Strip. They have built a very sophisticated recreational center in hopes that the hotels and casinos around would follow as soon as Arizona law allowed. The Center contained pools, spas, kitchen, dining area, public halls, gaming area, pro billiard room, and other facilities for a good army of gamblers and vacationers.

Well, the conservative state of Arizona balked, and the "enterprise" went bankrupt. The fancy facility in the middle of nowhere was auctioned to an entrepreneurial Chinese family from Los Angeles. They quickly built a fence, divided the land into small parcels around the Center, and leased them to the Snow Birds to put cute park models on these parcels. By the time when I saw this place, more than half of the parcels were occupied, and Siesta looked like a very comfortable place for happy senior citizens. I was particularly captivated with this "overkill" recreational facility so much, that I bought one of the park models on the spot.

For about four years, we traveled back and forth between Rhode Island and Bullhead City. This turned out to be not easy for Mary. To maintain a big house, left alone in "wet" Rhode Island for the whole winter, was not a simple task, either. I was looking for a possibility to settle permanently in Arizona, despite the realization this would isolate me more from my family in the Northeast. Joe settled in New York, bought his apartment in Manhattan, and started to gain his experience as a producer in the field of advertisement. Lora was also planning to move to New York as soon as Myron graduated from high school and moved to the college of his choice. My major concern was still the same—how to save my marriage. At the same time I had to make my loss of family contacts less painful by visiting the Northeast and keeping myself intellectually busy, physically active and esthetically stimulated.

The place, seemingly perfect to satisfy this set of conditions, was Sun Lagos, a very unique new community in Fort Mohave, 10 miles south from Bullhead City. Fort Mohave was a fast growing golfing Mecca of Arizona, and Sun Lagos was its logical center. The gated community of Sun Lagos was built around the cascade of three artificial lakes with a multitude of coves and canals, and with houses situated on their banks. The community had a clubhouse, pool, spa, tennis courts, fitness room, and everything else for active life. This was the place we decided to buy our permanent house. I would be happy enough, though, in my park model at Siesta. But for Mary, this would mean elimination of lifelong accumulated "stuff," mostly never used. The big house in Sun Lagos would solve this problem. Would it take care of a bunch of others?

After a long and arduous move, I was breaking my back in what was becoming a much too familiar mission—putting all this stuff neatly out of site, probably not to ever be seen.

Someone asked Frank Lloyd Wright, when he built his famous Arizona retreat: "You have lots of nice little shelves and niches for souvenirs in your retreat. Why haven't you designed any storage space?" Wright replied: "Storage is for things you never need." Well, Mary was determined to defeat Wright's wisdom once more.

Something almost unthinkable began to cross my mind: "Was this quarter of a century of my marriage just one huge mistake? Here we are—two people so different in family backgrounds—facing a terrible paradox: the Western open society, fostering tightly sealed family of denial and brutal abuse, vs. open family of love and care in a closed totalitarian state. It's a good piece of thinking for an army of sociologists and psychologists"

Once, when we still dating, Mary asked me, "What was a single thing you valued the most in your life?"

"Love," I said. "It's the purpose of life."

"What attracted you to me the most?" I asked in turn.

"The way you valued love" she answered.

How ironic was this answer, coming from someone, whose very concept of love was severely challenged by brutal abuse! Mary liked to be loved and taken care of—it made her feel secure and comfortable. But did she know how to love? Did she know how to fight for it at the time of danger? She didn't move a finger to save it, along with our marriage.

The fresh, crisp evening of this early March was exceptionally quiet. "Let's go for stargazing, Apry," said I to a little creature wagging his puffy tale—he was ready to go with me to the very edge of the Universe, no weather questioned, no questions asked. We climbed the spiral stairs on the roof deck. A new moon showed its razor-thin saddle; ready to follow the sun, already hidden behind the wavy range of the Dead Mountains on the Californian side. The Boundary Cone Mountain and the Black Mountains behind it on the opposite, the Arizonian, side of the horizon faintly reflected light of the new-born beauty. The endless black sky, crowded with billions and billions of stars and mirrored by the surface of the lake below, looked like a velvet carpet spread with diamonds. The stars were so large and bright, so incredibly close, that I fought the urge to jump off the deck and grab one of them. The feeling was familiar. It was pretty much like on that fateful flight to Vienna in May of 1977. Only then I resisted the urge to jump on the clouds beneath and roll in them in ecstasy. The "virtual reality" here was so surreal . . . it took my breath away.

"Only in Arizona! Only here the endless time can stop just like that in the middle of the run," blinked it in my mind. "Resume your count, Republic of Magic. *Only, please . . . start now from that Vienna flight again, would you? I promise, though, to stick with my favorite leitmotif this time—I sure have learned some hard lessons of history.*"

epilogue

"Peace is normally a great good, and normally it coincides with righteousness, but it is righteousness and not peace which should bind conscience of a nation as it should bind conscience of an individual; and neither a nation nor an individual can surrender to another's keeping."

THEODORE ROOSEVELT

I finished the story of my hero's life on one breath—with, of course, countless corrections after. It came out, in my view, as an optimistic testimony of flight to a freedom; of adaptation and professional success on a background of personal drama of love, abuse and sacrifice. It's a story of an ordinary man and his family, born on both sides of the ideological divide, the people of keen sense of good and wrong, of appreciation of their new country and its culture, the people of aversion to rare manifestation of bad choices in their ranks.

Now I am working on the final touches and thinking: "Have I, as a writer, fulfilled my promise to trust *a material presented by my hero and keep him from judgment?* Have I let the reader see only the hard and undeniable facts of my hero's life on both sides of the Iron Curtain and draw the own conclusions?" Naturally, I have no answer to these questions. It's the reader's job.

But as an American, as *an author of the book* and citizen of the world, I feel free from any emotional restraint. I think I have never been a cold and impassive observer of the great historical events of my time, and I would *never let anyone I touch* forget lessons of history we learned. America welcomed my family, just like Jay's, and has made me a proud citizen of the best country in the world. And I owe her at least as much as complete honesty and regards to her very best interests. It's *my* country for some time now and forever, *in sickness and health.* So, if someone labels me "crazy" in connection with my patriotism, I would gladly take it as a compliment.

I am also a capitalist—I proudly manage my IRA, and so far I succeed to cover my modest expenses and preserve my little nest egg. But it seems strange that every time when Chuck Schumer, my favorite senator from New York makes some *schume* ("noise" in Russian, by an amazing coincidence) about how bad we are doing, the financial market slides. And when he takes a break, market slowly comes back. This consistency looks like a great opportunity to me. Would you, Chuck, please, just give me a wink when you are planning next press conference, so I can make some adjustments in my investment? I would appreciate it and hope this innocent trick is not in the law books yet and wouldn't be qualified as insider trading.

As a person who spent a life time on both sides of ideological divide, and had an opportunity to take a good hard look, compare and reflect, I have something to say both the young liberals and their politically charged spiritual leaders. *Those of them* who don't realize what is at stake in our fight with modern Totalitarianism, those who *just don't get it again*, please feel free to use my shoes for 30 years or so—the time span of my adult Russian experience—just to clear your minds a little bit. These shoes are one-size-fits-all and a good school for everyone blessed with neurons in their brains. With all due respect, watching you, guys, helped me a great deal to put things in historical perspective, sort out what you preach, admire what you often hate, and choose proper tune for this book. Just please keep in mind that the Bolshevik revolution in Russia started with innocent liberalism of the well-meaning idealistic intelligentsia. It ended with ugly totalitarianism of political Mafia, killing those liberals first, and then far more than 50 million others. *This is an undeniable historical outcome of ultra left utopia.*

A couple days ago, watching TV, I stumbled into a mosaic of clips. Someone has compiled it just for me, helping me to put the final touch on my story.

On the first clip I recognized the face of the famous entertainer Harry Belafonte. I always liked him and whistled lots of his tunes. Now, however, he was doing something not quite amusing—he was warmly hugging Chavez, this thug of Venezuela, and calling our Home Security Department "the Nazi Gestapo." I wondered what epithet he would find for the same department if it, God forbid, missed critical information and failed to prevent destruction of ... oh, let's say, the Brooklyn Bridge, or any other symbol of our pride and national might. And all this *cozy cuddling* was taking place in time of war, when American soldiers were dying for the very liberty that Mr. Belafonte was "defending" so eloquently.

As I remember, he hugged Fidel Castro, the "master" of

Cuba, too, and with an equal enthusiasm. I wondered, if he found Bin Laden covered with lime and lice in his "cave palace," or Saddam Hussein in his "rat hole residence," would he kiss their dusty shoulders first or rather something else more sexy? If Stalin rose from his grave, handsome and powerful, would Belafonte, this epitome of "patriotism and intelligence," resist smearing his saliva all over the bushy mustache of the very bloodiest monster in the human history? Unlike some other pathetically immature and ignorant "thinkers," confused and completely "Sarandonned," the good entertainers and bad communicators, would Mr. Belafonte ever come out with any suggestion or solution? If he runs out of *ultra-left* sentiments, would he pass up an opportunity to pull on his head that fancy fez of, at this time the *ultra-right* Muslim fundamentalist, Louis Farakhan? We remember lessons of science and history: The extremes, just like those Lobachevsky's parallels, always meet, and as I understand ... *never in a good place.*

The second clip was about an admitted terrorist and legalized American, Zacharia Moussaui, using the public podium to profess his hate for his country and his readiness to cut every American head he can put his hands on, with, pardon, a serrated knife, just to make his victims suffer longer. I saw pictures of such executions committed with a cheer of the *"righteous"* crowd in the Taliban times. And, somewhere on a background of this clip, of course is ... Oh, here he is, the well-spoken and well imbedded into an educational system, full of hate for America, *Professor* Churchill, defending the "First" from possible assault.

The third clip was even more puzzling. It showed millions of illegal emigrants from Mexico on the streets of large American cities. They carried Mexican flags, wiping their shoes on Stars and Stripes, and angrily demanded to open borders for the sake of *bloodless* victory in a New Mexican-American war. And on a background of it I could recognize a bunch of our distinguished politicians, scared to lose a few votes needed to keep them in the office.

And the last clip logically concluded the whole series. It showed the picture of the Iranian President Ahmadinejad, pledging—the day after he reaffirmed his nuclear ambitions—to wipe Israel from the world map and showing his middle finger to the ever-impotent United Nations. He wouldn't have to nuke Israel by himself, though—it would be too dangerous. He would rather provide next TV clip for us all to "enjoy"—Bin Laden or his successor with a nuke on his side and the poster of smoky Ground Zero, attached to the wall of his cave, saying: "You guys got a good chunk of New York real estate and the whole area around it wasted for a century. We, with help of Allah, will make every big city of yours to smoke and stink like that, unless you convert to Islam and follow laws of Shariah and customs of Taliban." And then, Professor Churchill, you wouldn't have to worry about freedom of speech. When some day, hypothetically, they drag your mighty body out of your complacent university and cut your head off with serrated knife, they wouldn't even care to ask which side you were on.

Oh, by the way, don't we know how the first head of the Soviet Socialist State, Vladimir Ilyich Lenin, officially called his policy of struggle against pro-Western democratic movement in Russia during October Revolution? Exactly! The *"Red Terror."*

Anyone knows that we didn't ask for this war. We were attacked everywhere, even on our soil. We are fighting this war now on their soil to never have it on ours anymore. So, a "fair political justification" for our response is just as relevant as an old stale joke; the question of where, when and how to respond is now a matter of self-defense at this point; and the consequences of non-action and defeat in this war are beyond any calculation.

To the benefit of the modern anti-war movement: The lessons of history can't be clearer: Defeat in war leads to the anarchy and turmoil. Russian defeat in the war with Japan led to the first bloody and brutally subdued Communist revolution of 1905. Its defeat in WWI led to a Bolshevik Revolution in October 1917—we all know the result of it. The humiliation of Germany after WWI led to rise of Nazism … and we know the result of it, too. There has been only one country in the world that never needed the war, never started any without blatant provocation, and was always critically instrumental in creating peaceful and prosperous zones around the world. And this country is *mine now*.

Yet, another lesson of history we often tend to forget—the popular Russian proverb: "Nyet Proroka v Svoyem Otechestve," which in English sounds like: "There can never be any prophet in the Country of my own." Abraham Lincoln was "trashed" by a good majority of Americans and gave his life for the Country he served. He transformed slavery to freedom and saved the integrity of our Country.

Ronald Reagan was ridiculed as "imbecile" when he allegedly tricked one of our enemies to fund a demise of another one. He was called the "Mad Hawk," when he armed Europe, threatened a deployment of the "Star War" System, demanded demolition of the Berlin Wall, and buried the Soviet Empire. All of these visionaries made their mistakes, and lots of them, but history put their vision first. As we all know, one who does nothing makes no mistakes.

Now we are in a new war, this time against invisible enemy,

with no real estate and no regards to life, the enemy living like a parasite on the body of rogue States. This war calls for a new approach, for bold and often controversial thinking, in order to protect the world from assured destruction. And over again some are ready to undermine the effort and cut the limbs we are sitting on. "Complacency" is the word to describe it.

For someone who isn't aware of these historical lessons, it's time to go to the library, switch TV set off the Game Show for a while, or just shut up. The others, however, who know these facts but hurts his or her Country in time of war any way, may, in my opinion, very well be qualified for liability.

All those questions of historic significance and personal observation run in my mind, while I was watching these clips. I looked at the TV screen with a sinking feel of nausea in my stomach.... . And with all my limited skills, with all the piety I could only master—considering my forty-five years of atheistic sterilization under the "Dictatorship of Proletariat"—I prayed:

"Bless, the Lord, this gentle country of ours, and show us, please, how to solve our *dilemma*, which Joseph Stalin, Adolph Hitler and Saddam Hussein would never even begin to contemplate. Tell us how to fight our sworn enemies often imbedded in our midst and armed to the teeth with bomb belts, box cutters and serrated knives, and desperate for any means of mass destruction—and at the same time survive the muddy waves of vicious attack of some of our own "citizens." How to do that without losing our liberty and integrity in the process, without using methods of our enemies, and of course without sending those wretched *"citizens" of ours* ... to Siberia ... in the winter ... by foot ... with their (pardon!) 'schtinken' pants off?

[1] war lord, *russ*

[2] Jewish ghetto town

[3] that's all right, *russ*

[4] Jew (derog), *russ*

[5] peasant house, *russ*

[7] fake show (slang), *russ*